DATACLOUD

TOWARD A NEW THEORY OF ONLINE WORK

NEW DIMENSIONS IN COMPUTERS AND COMPOSITION

Gail E. Hawisher and Cynthia L. Selfe, editors

Datacloud: Toward a New Theory of Online Work
Johndan Johnson-Eilola

At Play in the Fields of Writing: A Serio-Ludic Rhetoric
Albert Rouzie

Sustainable Computer Environments: Cultures of Support in English
Studies and Language Arts
Richard Selfe

Doing Literacy Online: Teaching, Learning, and Playing
in an Electronic World
Ilana Snyder and Catherine Beavis (eds.)

forthcoming

Digital Youth: Technologies and the Future of Literacy
Jonathan Alexander

Role Play: Distance Learning and the Teaching of Writing
Jonathan Alexander and Marcia Dickson (eds.)

Lingua Franca: Towards a Rhetoric of New Media
Colin Brooke

Aging Literacies: Training and Development Challenges for Faculty
Angela Crow

Labor, Writing Technologies and the Shaping of Composition
in the Academy
Pamela Takayoshi and Patricia Sullivan (eds.)

Integrating Hypertextual Subjects: Computers, Composition, Critical
Literacy and Academic Labor
Robert Samuels

DATACLOUD

TOWARD A NEW THEORY OF ONLINE WORK

Johndan Johnson-Eilola
Clarkson University

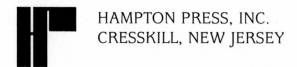

HAMPTON PRESS, INC.
CRESSKILL, NEW JERSEY

Printed in the United States of America

Library of Congress Cataloging-in-Publication Data

Johnson-Eilola, Johndan
    Datacloud : toward a new theory of online work / Johndan Johnson-Eilola
        p. cm. -- (New dimensions in computers and composition)
    Includes bibliographical references and index.
    ISBN 1-57273-634-8 -- ISBN 1-57273-635-6
      1. Information technology--Social aspects. 2. Human-computer
    interaction. I. Title. II. Series.

    T58.5.J647 2005
    303.48'33--dc22

                                      2005040334

Hampton Press, Inc.
23 Broadway
Cresskill, NJ 07626

CONTENTS

List of Figures

Contents

List of Tables

ACKNOWLEDGMENTS

As with the rest of my life, *Datacloud* is a dynamic and contingent articulation—indeed, an ongoing disarticulation and rearticulation.

Words of encouragement, challenge, and humor (in no particular order): Stuart Selber, Steve Doheny-Farina, Geoff Farina, Amy Kimme Hea, Anne Wysocki, Dickie Selfe, Barbara Mirel, Dan Dullea, Brent Faber, Bill Hart-Davison, Brad Mehlenbacher; Diane Davis, Erin Smith, Mark Crane, Michael Joyce, Jim Porter, Dennis Lynch, and Clay Spinuzzi.

In addition to generous and challenging feedback from colleagues and students at Clarkson University, I received financial support from Clarkson University, including assistance from the School of Liberal Arts, the School of Arts and Sciences, the Eastman Kodak Center for Excellence in Communication, and the Department of Technical Communications, which have variously funded travel to present and discuss portions of *Datacloud* at various academic and industry conferences.

For supplying some important resource materials on The Flaming Lips Brad Beasley (*The Flaming Lips Have Landed*) and new media composition, Todd Taylor (*New Media Convention Live*).

A majority of this book was written on the road. Important discussions and feedback came about during invited lectures and workshops at the University of Vermont, the University of Arizona, Case Western Reserve University, Michigan Technological University, University of Illinois at Urbana-Champain, St. Lawrence University, Illinois Institute of Technology, Nouspace, the University of Texas at Austin, the University of Washington, Rensselaer Polytechnic Institute (over email and speakerphone with the TextTome Reading Group), and the University of South Florida. Thanks to all.

Research participants: Brent Faber, David Dies, Ryan McDougal, Carolyn Eilola, Jay Goodell, Marcel Cote III, and several anonymous subjects.

Sound reinforcement: The Flaming Lips; DJ Logic; Wilco; Medeski, Martin, and Wood; Steve Earle; Steinski; Lucinda Williams; Guided By

Voices; Tom Waits; Camper Van Beethoven; PJ Harvey; Bardo Pond; Chet Baker; Paul Westerberg; Kelly Joe Phelps; Bark; Soul Coughing; Ryan Adams; Capt. Beefheart and the Magic Band; Joe Pass; Sonic Youth; Tool; Robert Johnson; The Drive-By Truckers; Neil Young; Nine Inch Nails; The White Stripes; Ornette Coleman; The Pixies; Peanut Butter Wolf; Gov't Mule; Grandmaster Flash; Gillian Welch and David Rawlings; WTSC; iTunes; GarageBand; BitTorrent; LimeWire; Sharing the Groove; and a cast of thousands.

Cindy Selfe and Gail Hawisher, who continue to encourage and publish my work. Barbara Bernstein at Hampton Press provided invaluable assistance in guiding the ragged manuscript into publication.

As always, Underdog and Spork.

I know I've forgotten someone. I owe you a beer.

Written (in no particular order) in Saint Regis Falls, NY; Saranac Lake, NY; Chicago, IL; Normal, IL; Little Switzerland, NC; Burlington, VT; Tucson, AZ; Cleveland, OH; Houghton, MI: West Lafayette, IN; Potsdam, NY; Canton, NY; Tampa, FL; Austin, TX; Urbana, IL; and various airport boarding areas and in flight.

0

INTRODUCTION:
ERRATIC TRAJECTORIES

You just . . . play.
—Carolyn Eilola

We talk in fevered voices of the computer revolution, but the shape and tra-jectory of that revolution are only now becoming clear at the fringes. Although computers now touch our lives in substantial and ubiquitous ways, their impact has remained relatively benign. The ways in which we work and live now include digital components—and computers are now everywhere and constitute relatively large portions of our everyday work and the global economy—but our processes and structures for working and living have not radically changed. Microsoft Word provides us with a faster, more flexible typewriter; Adobe Photoshop offers us a wonderful array of photographic darkroom tools (even if many of us do not recognize them as such); and RealMedia streams provide us with radio or television stations.

In short, until now the computer revolution may only, as Zuboff (1989) put it nearly two decades ago, be a "revolution" in the sense of revolving around a point, faster and faster.

In one way of thinking, the revolution is no longer a coherent, discrete event, but instead a dispersed network of subtle, yet profound changes in patterns of working, living, and communicating. Surprisingly, these shifts are not occurring within cutting-edge research and development centers or think tanks. Although such sites might provide the genesis of new forms and processes of working and living, it is in the real world—on the street, in the workplace, and in the home—that change begins to take hold. For radical change, by definition, is not simply a speeding up of existing

1

processes or an increase in efficiency of existing structures, but a major reworking of them. In fact at first such shifts are not likely to be easily identifiable as important changes, although they occur in a multitude of disparate locations. Frequently, these changes look chaotic only to those clinging to old ways of working. The interesting things are happening in the interstices rather than the edges.

For example, a little over 5 years ago, I watched as my daughter, Carolyn, then 7, played a computer game called *Per.Oxyd* (1995) that she had downloaded from a shareware site (Fig. 0.1). The interface sported almost no explanatory text or conventionally meaningful icons; the brief instructions were written in German (which neither of us could read).[1] She was not intimidated, confused, or annoyed; she seemed to consider the lack of instructions part of the game. She merely started the game and began clicking on objects on the dense, multicolored screen. Within moments, she became absorbed in this world of pulsing icons and buzzing tones, playing for hours, moving from level to level in a bizarre pattern of changing actions and reactions that I was completely incapable of following. I came of age in the Atari generation and considered myself relatively adept at the world of videogames, but my age was showing. I was struck by her ability to cope with a game that appeared to have no preset rules or goals, as many of us are struck by the abilities of children to adapt to new ways of playing, working, and living. Videogames have always prioritized an experiential nature, but the games I used to play possessed simple, rel-

Fig. 0.1. Screenshot from *Per.Oxyd*.

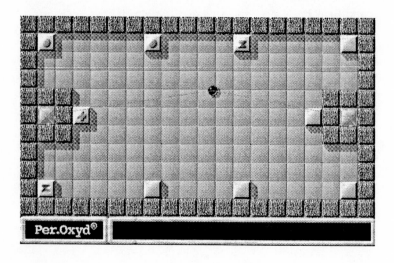

atively static sets of rules—an easy set of discoverable rules per level. In *Per.Oxyd*, contingency ruled.

I recorded part of our later conversation about the game for a chapter I was writing for an edited collection on computers and literacy (Johnson-Eilola, 1997):

Johndan: How do you know which blocks to hit?
C: I just . . . hit them.
[...]
J: So how do you figure out what the rules are?
C: Just play.
J: Just play? And then what happens?
C: You just . . . play.

Over the next 5 years, I began to see this sort of activity—contingent, experimental, loosely goal-driven, playful—in an increasing number of situations—not only games, but all around me. At least part of this shift, I argue, is due to the dramatic increase in the amount of information we deal with on a daily basis. I am not talking simply about the growth of online spaces or media, although those are related issues. Rather, how we live has changed: We have come to work with information as a primary environment and resource. Whereas the industrial age focused on the production of concrete objects, the information age focuses on the production of information. In this epoch, information workers do not merely use information, they *inhabit* it.

What struck me about the the conversation with Carolyn—and conversations with other people, ranging from discussions with students using search engines and Web site designers working on large sites to observations of musicians composing in nonlinear audio editing environments—was that the patterns of working seemed different than those with which I had experience, those that our existing models of education and work suggested. Rather than establishing frameworks and ground rules early on, users in these environments learned—and created—rules on the fly. Rather than understanding creativity as the inspired production of solitary genius, these users manipulated preexisting data, filtering, cutting, pasting, and moving. Rather than seeing information as something they needed to master and contain, they saw information as a rich field in which to work. I was struck by the possibilities of computer use as something that broke open and radically transformed traditional ways of working and living.

* * *

The sheer amount of information in our current lives—the infosphere that we individually inhabit[2]—threatens our ability to sort it into neat categories, to summarize it in simple terms. Those necessities are falling by the wayside. Today many of us thrive on information overload: e-mail, cell phone, satellite TV, instant messenger (IM). We live in a cloud of data, the *datacloud*—a shifting and only slightly contingently structured information space. In that space, we work with information, rearranging, filtering, breaking down, and combining. We are not looking for simplicity, but interesting juxtapositions and commentaries. This is the vague shape and erratic trajectory of the coming revolution.

This book investigates ways of understanding and intervening in that revolution. Working recursively between practices and theories, I attempt to build a rough framework and practice for recognizing and critically analyzing important and ongoing shifts in the way we work, communicate, and live, particularly (but not limited to) our growing online lives. In addition, I mobilize several related critical methods for constructing active and productive responses to those shifts.

This selection of theories and disciplines will likely strike many readers as odd or ill advised. The two primary themes in this work, for example, are symbolic-analytic work and articulation theory. The former comes from contemporary economic and labor research produced by Robert Reich, former U.S. Secretary of Labor; the latter grows out of the work of Stuart Hall, British cultural studies theorist and neomarxist/post-postmodernist philosopher. But although these two strands seem incapable of being woven into any sort of coherent tapestry, the threads that I pull from them reenforce rather than contest each other. Each theorist works to understand dramatic changes in contemporary culture brought about by the rise of the information economy, late capitalism, and postmodernism (although Reich would probably use the term *postindustrial capitalism*).

Similarly, in this work, I tend to equate *material production* (building concrete things like Ford F-150s or Cuisinart coffeemakers) with *symbolic production* (building symbolic things like strategic reports on the economies of a specific market niche or posts to a Weblog). The ability to move around two discrete objects on a computer screen turns into an aptitude for postmodernist collage, the juxtaposition of elements that does not merely link both, but deconstructs the stability of each object's meaning. The whole is more than—and less than—the sum of its parts.

Purists in ethnography, linguistics, economics, or interface design might shudder at the collapse of levels here. Yet if *Datacloud* is about anything, it is about the postmodernist ways in which symbols are now a class of material objects, conceptual objects, with market value, social force, and dimension.

The breadth and diversity of *Datacloud* means that there are not (and probably can never be) simple answers or guaranteed solutions. Indeed to some extent, this whole project involves the acknowledgment that life is not something to be solved, but engaged, challenged, transformed, and, in the end, lived.

Notes

1. *Per.Oxyd.* appears to have originally been written in the United States; it is possible that Carolyn somehow found a version localized for German users.
2. As I refer to it later, the information that articulates us on an ongoing basis.

1

REARTICULATIONS: THE CHANGING SHAPES OF COMPUTER SPACES

Turntablism: [T]he use of a phonograph turntable as a tool to create music, not just to play it. In essence, turntablism is music based on sound manipulation. It centers on sounds called "scratches" that can be produced through the manipulation of sounds recorded onto records.
—Gadd (2004)

An articulation is . . . the form of the connection that can be made between two different elements, under certain conditions. It is a link-age that is not necessary, determined, absolute and essential for all time. You have to ask, under what circumstances can a connection be forged or made? So the so-called "unity" of a discourse is really the articulation of different, distinct elements which can be rearticulated in different ways because they have no necessary "belongingness." The "unity' which matters is a linkage between that articulated discourse and the social forces with which it can, under certain historical condi-tions, but need not necessarily, be connected.
—Hall (1989, p. 141)

We have been criticized for overquoting literary authors. But when one writes, the only question is which other machine the literary machine can be plugged into, must be plugged into in order to work.
—Deleuze and Guattari (1987, p. 4)

ALMOST UNNOTICED:
UNDERSTANDING THE FUTURE NOW

This is a book about the future contained within the present, almost unnoticed.

We devote much energy to thinking about radical change, about paint-ing a wonderfully alien future made of light and air—a vision that seems to draw more than a little of its shape from Fritz Lang's *Metropolis*. Wearable computers. Nanoscale technologies. Immersive virtual workspaces.

There is nothing wrong with these visions. They provide us with some-thing to think toward—new ways to think, work, and live. Yet the noise we make about these technologies frequently blinds us to more profound shifts in our culture—changes that may have, in the long run, a larger effect on our futures as well as our current lives. Slow, small, and wide-ranging transformations in the nature of communication, in environments for work and learning, and in our ways of relating to each other and to technology— these transformations occur among us on a daily basis almost without our recognizing them.

Some of these changes, like the explosion of information in our every-day lives, we[1] tend to cope with as best we can while yearning for an ear-lier, simpler life. Some of these changes, like the development of graphical computer interfaces, we have learned to take for granted. Some of these changes, like the ubiquitous use of instant messaging (IM) programs and moblogs, we toy with but consider to be *only* a toy, a cheap imitation of real, substantive communication.

And maybe it's so: Toys have always been among the most telling and prescient signals of a culture's histories and futures: Monopoly, Barbie, and Grand Theft Auto: Vice City all suggest useful critical inquiries into class, gender, race, and technology. Nursery rhymes only seem innocent. The singsong

> Ring around the rosie
> Pocketful of posies
> Ashes, ashes
> We all fall down

provides a cynical commentary—an ironic user's manual—to life and death during the time of the bubonic plague: hold a bouquet to one's nose to combat the stench of the dead and to purify the air of infectious spirits; burn the corpses; in the end, all perish.

Fig. 1.1. Laura Burstein's moblog (< http://lburstein.textamerica.com/ >)

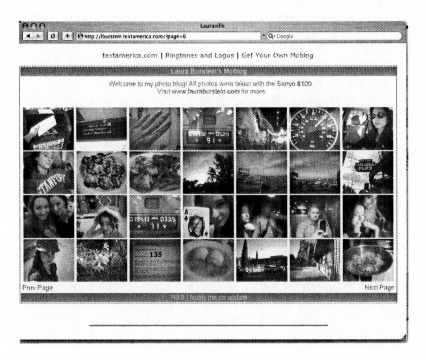

Like nursery rhymes and children's toys, many of the technologies and activities I discuss in *Datacloud* seem, at first glance, to be irrelevant, annoying, off topic, or innocuous. Yet, as I demonstrate, many of these conceptual objects are sites of important cultural shifts. In this analysis, I attempt to move out of the realm of simple cause and effect toward an understanding of culture and technology as contingent, multidimensional, fragmented, and constructed in local uses rather than universal determinations. We are in a networked culture, both in the sense of communication networks and concepts, objects, and subjects being constructed by interconnected social and technical forces. As such, examining even apparently trivial activities like IM can help us to better understand, learn from, shape, and extend these cultural shifts in productive ways.

The possibility of agency within these apparently chaotic contexts requires us to adjust some of our assumptions. Our existing models of both communication and work tend to support relatively linear, orderly, modernistic activities and objects. Work in the information age, however, increasingly requires a different approach—one that we have succeeded in cobbling together, but with only partial and limited successes. We rarely consider the possibility that the gaps between old and new ways are not necessarily flaws, that the gaps may be opportunities, suggestions about new methods for understanding work. We might be excused for failing to consider these new possibilities because our existing frameworks do not allow us to understand communication, work, and play in these ways. What we thought was noise in the channel turns out to be another signal— one richer in possibilities than the one to which we're currently accustomed. From a datacloud way of thinking, we need simultaneous access to multiple channels, information overload be damned (Fig. 1.2).

Fig. 1.2. The man who fell to earth (Deeley, Spikings, & Roeg, 1976).

To expand the availability of powerful new ways of understanding and working within information, we need to reconstruct—rearticulate—what we mean when we talk about communicating and working. In an information age, these activities are not about order or production, but about manipulation, contingency, semirandom movement, and reinterpretation.

It is commonplace to say that we live in an information society. We understand, at some level, that culture in the United States and other countries has shifted away from the production and circulation of objects and toward the production and circulation of information: industrial economy to information and knowledge economy. Whereas the rise of the industrial era had Chaplin's (1936) satire, *Modern Times*, the decline has Moore's (1989) *Roger and Me*. Looking askance at the rise of the information era, we have films such as Terry Gilliam's dystopian *Brazil* (Milchan & Gilliam, 1985), where information, communication, and knowledge work become oppressive forces in their own right.

Consider the historical trajectory in the construction of dystopias between two of these films: Chaplin's *Modern Times*, the classic comedy on industrialization (Fig. 1.3), versus Gilliam's *Brazil*, an ironic dystopia (Fig. 1.4). *Modern Times* pits the hapless Chaplin against the machinery and management of the factory, an ordeal that contorts his body into inhuman shapes and speeds up his actions until they break down. Machines literally consume Chaplin, integrating him within their inner workings.

Fig. 1.3. Chaplin in the machine (1936).

Brazil's dystopia, a film made at the early edge of the information age, provides a different order: The machine still occasionally consumes bodies, but its primary workings involve breakdowns in communication. The main narrative arc of the film is launched when a bug's corpse[2] causes an error during the printing of arrest warrants. Even office work within *Brazil* involves convoluted and dysfunctional communication situations, ranging from miniscule computer monitors (requiring enormous magnifying lenses) to Victorian-style communication tubes backing up.

Fig. 1.4. Office technologies in *Brazil* (Milchan & Gilliam, 1985).

The dual climactic points of the film are both communication breakdowns: Resistance fighter Harry Tuttle is engulfed in a sea of windblown papers and newsprint and literally disappears into these scattered texts, swept away; Everyman Sam Lowry retreats from a tortuous interrogation—at the hands of his boss—into a utopian dreamworld.

The design of sets in *Brazil* points to one of the difficulties involved in understanding revolution from the inside: The familiarity of our everyday lives tends to desensitize us to those very forces that we live within. Hence, Gilliam's sets portray a dystopian information culture that looks remarkably like the art deco designs of the industrial age, forcing us back from a futuristic, clean information culture.

Fig. 1.5. Sam Lowry escapes (Milchan & Gilliam, 1985).

The information society in *Brazil* and other works of popular imagination represents something simultaneously terrifying and amusing: We laugh darkly while we attempt simply to survive. One instant we are shown images of those who have successfully managed to ride the wave (Microsoft's *"Where Do You Want to Go Today?"* promises to take us anywhere if we can just keep our directories and bookmarks in order) and the next instant we read stories of dot.com millionaires suddenly penniless when the edifices they built collapse ("W*hat's the big surprise? Their castles were built of information instead of bricks and mortar!"*).

Films such as *Minority Report,* Stephen Spielberg's (Molen, Curtis, Parkes, de Bont, and Spielberg, 2002) adaptation of the text by Philip K. Dick, provide a new way to understand how our culture views the workplace.[3] Whereas work in *Modern Times* and *Brazil* follows dystopic lines, *Minority Report's* John Adams' work relies on a futuristic computer interface that supports the retrieval and movement of masses of information (Fig. 1.6).

The interface, designed with the assistance of long-time information age activist John Perry Barlow, offers one near vision of interfaces that support information work: working with massive amounts of information from disparate sources, applying filters, manipulating video and point of view— activities that I discuss later as primary examples of work in the datacloud.

Fig. 1.6. Working the datacloud in *Minority Report* (Molen, Curtis, Parkes, e bont, & Spielberg, 2002).

Viewer

Additionally, all three of these films document the movement from modernism to postmodernism: *Modern Times,* with its emphasis on the control of the body in space in time (the factory line, Chaplin being integrated physically into the machinery); and *Brazil,* oscillating between subjects consumed by machinery (Jack Buttle's arrest; Jack Tuttle's consumption by stray newspapers) and conquering both space and time (Jack's imagined superhero, which escapes the reality of the film). *Minority Report* then tends toward the occupation of both space and time, with precognizant mutants allowing the prevention of crimes before they are ever committed. In this context, vision becomes crucial, as information is surfaced, n-dimensional rather than simply a temporal thread. Citizens (and transgressors) are identified by eye scans—a technology that requires Jack to have his eyes surgically replaced to escape unjust capture. Near the end of the film, Jack frequently refers explicitly to vision: "Can you see?" and "How could I not have seen this?"

The visual has long occupied film—its main distinction from other media such as radio was its visual aspect—but contemporary parables frequently emphasize the power of vision to understand and control space and subjectivity. In *A Clockwork Orange*, miscreant Alex is "cured" by forced viewing of filmed violence (Fig. 1.7).

Blade Runner, another film based on a Philip K. Dick story, hinges on the connection between vision and subjectivity: Artificial humans, *replicants*, are identified primarily through the Voigt-Kampff test, which measures (among other things) pupil and iris fluctuations in response to various questions posed about situations involving violence against animals (many species of which are extinct in this futuristic setting) (Fig. 1.8). Replicants apparently cannot empathize with animals, and their eyes betray that failure.

Replicants fail to be human in another key way in *Blade Runner*: They have very limited lifespans, preprogrammed to die after a certain number of years. Humans, much more flexible in their lifespans (even if more open to chance violence often at the hands of replicants in the film), control the replicants through the human control of time.

The equation between vision and postmodernism is not always so clean (*The Wizard of Oz*, for example, emphasizes vision as a way to control space and destiny through the Wicked Witch of the West's crystal ball), but in general we observe a shift away from a focus on time and toward a focus on space in our cultures. This shift is neither inherently good nor bad, although it is frequently cast as negative by those who feel more firmly entrenched in history. Until we can understand the broader implications of

Fig. 1.7. **"And vidi films I did." Alex's cure in *A Clockwork Orange* (Kubrick, 1971).**

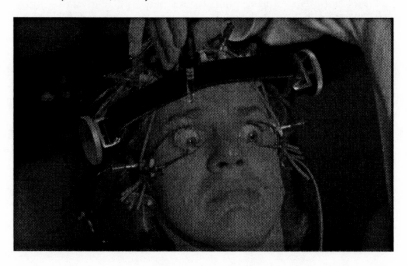

Fig. 1.8.   **Voight-Kampff testing in *Blade Runner* (Deeley & Scott,
1982).**

this shift, we are be unable to participate fully, actively, and critically within this emerging context.

   Datacloud occupies neither end of the continuum between utopia and
dystopia. Paradoxically, it also avoids simply sitting in the middle, paralyzed
between two extremes. Instead the situations and events I discuss here
move back and forth between those two poles, attempting to construct a
three-dimensional space in relation to but perpendicular to the other two
dimensions. In fact most of the things I use as examples in the book are
everyday events, some slightly less common than others, but all the stuff of
workplaces and classrooms rather than high-end research and development
(R&D) labs. I would be overstating the case to say that we never see these
things. Oddly, although these cases surround us, we often fail to see their
significance. When we do notice them, it is often with a feeling of annoyance or superiority: there is just something not quite *right* about them. They
look like games or mistakes, breakdowns or misdirections.

   They are breakdowns. That is their power. Breakdown is the first
phase of rebuilding.

BREAKDOWN AND RECOMBINATION

These examinations work from the premise that our existing lives, our patterns of working, living, and communicating and our relationships to each other in all of those areas, are dynamic processes of ongoing construction and reconstruction. In this realm, technologies are not isolated and neutral things that can be moved from context to context without change. To take an obvious linguistic example, consider the pronoun *I*, which changes meaning in big ways depending on context. Not merely depending on *who* utters the self-referential, but whether that bodied person speaks for (as it were) him or herself versus an organization, he or she is reciting lines in a play, or he or she is singing the alphabet song. In other words, context is crucial. Language, far from being neutral, has material effects in that meanings provide cultures with methods for operating. As such, language shapes our development and use of technologies, our ways of working, and more. Recursively, our development and uses of those technologies are intimately bound up with how language is used and changed.

The term *computer* has shifted dramatically over the last century. Webster's 1913 Dictionary defined a *computer* as, "One who computes"—in other words, the term was a job description rather than a technological artifact. Only in the mid-20th century was the term applied to early versions of the technology that eventually was called a computer. Clearly the meaning of the term *computer* in 1950 meant something different than it does today or even 20 years ago. On the one hand, there are key similarities (or as Stuart Hall put it, "lines of tendential force" [cited in Grossberg, 1986, p. 142]) that strongly influence the construction of specific technologies along somewhat generic lines. For example, what we call a *computer* today tends to include a keyboard, a mouse or trackpad, a color display device between 12 inches and 22 inches (measured diagonally), and so on. Yet 10 years ago, a mouse would not have been as strong a tendency in the articulation; 10 years from now, if voice recognition and transcription technology advance sufficiently, a keyboard might be missing. As an articulation, a computer tends to have certain features, but those features change over time and from location to location. Change is frequently difficult (especially for the stronger tendential forces), but both historical evidence as well as simultaneous variation show us that changes are possible.

Technological inventions are not simply dropped from the sky to dramatically and deterministically reshape our lives. Instead we integrate them into our specific, local situations. We create, import, use, and misuse them in wildly idiosyncratic ways—often for purposes their inventors never intended. That is not to say that some core, dispassionate self coldly determines how to live in the absence of any effect from the outside world. Quite the opposite: There is no core, dispassionate self, but only a network of social and technical forces constructing the I as an ongoing, contingent process, a useful fiction. That is not to say there is no I, but that the self arises as a meaningful construct only in the flux of those multiple forces.

As with words and people, interactions with technologies are also contingent, neither completely free nor completely bounded. A computer does not typically *force* us to act in a particular way (although some actions might be strongly *suggested* by how the computer is structured[5]), but we are also not free to make the computer do anything we imagine (although we do have an influence on how the computer works beyond what it explicitly suggests).

In *Datacloud*, I use two primary methods for understanding how people make meaning within their daily lives in information-saturated environments. The two methods or approaches come from different disciplines, but are nonetheless similar: articulation theory and symbolic-analytic work. I devote the second chapter to providing a more detailed account of these two components, but I briefly outline them here to highlight my intentions in bringing them together.

Articulation theory, the first component, comes from the field of cultural studies, where the theory and method emerged in the 1980s and 1990s primarily through the work of Stuart Hall as a way to understand the complex formatting of ideological subjects in contemporary culture. Most important, articulation theory offers a way to represent the possibility of *resistance* to dominant cultural formations. Articulation theory represents a response to traditional marxism, which tends to position citizens in capitalist cultures as completely determined by the ideological superstructures. Articulation theory also responds to postmodernism, which tends to represent people as increasingly and overwhelmingly fragmented by the breakdown in symbol systems that constitute contemporary culture. In other words, articulation theory accepts the breakdowns of contemporary culture, but also insists there *are* contingently coherent cultures and ongoing, constantly under identities.

Symbolic-analytic work, the second component of the framework I construct, emerged from the work of labor theorist Robert Reich in the 1990s. Less a method than a rough job description, symbolic-analytic work was used by Reich to describe the type of work done be a wide range of people in the burgeoning information economy. Symbolic-analytic workers, as the title suggests, manipulate symbols. This new classification comprises a host of cultural elite professionals: architects, systems analysts, investment bankers, research scientists, management consultants, and so on. Clearly not every member of these professions falls within the ranks of symbolic analysts, but the subgroup across each of these professions excels at working with information—not merely simplifying information to make it clear, but working *within* information, filtering, rearranging, transforming, and making connections to address specific, specialized problems. In other words—not Reich's words—symbolic analysts are people we might think of as *technical rhetoricians* working in the datacloud.

Admittedly, the fit between these two frameworks is an uneasy one. Articulation theory forefronts resistant, political stances that many (although not all) symbolic-analytic workers would vehemently protest. Yet that contradiction is also the reason to force them together: Articulation theory provides a method for politicizing symbolic-analytic work, whereas symbolic-analytic work provides vocational training for what too easily can devolve into liberal posturing. *Datacloud,* in one limited sense, is a job ad for information age cultural workers.

* * *

This book does not offer a complete history of the World Wide Web or the computer. In fact many of the specific divisions I discuss or dates of emergence might be contested in one direction or another. I am more interested here in examining the interaction between general trends—tendential forces—and specific articulations, in the ways that people understand, work with, and reconstruct technologies, and the ways that those activities both suggest and reflect changes in our cultures.

This project began as an examination of computer interfaces, the ways in which they structure work. I soon realized this research topic was far too narrow—interfaces only tell part of the story. As Mirel (2003) observed in her book on interfaces for complex problem solving,

> Complexity does not reside as a property in the data, in an external situation, or in a problem solver's cognitive profile alone. It is impossible to talk about complex problem solving separate from the interchanges that go on between problem solvers and their environments. . . .
>
> It is common in user-centered design to focus on people's activities in context. But this singular use of the term "context" is misleading. In real world activities, people act in a large number of contexts—contexts that are social, technological, organizational, physical, cultural, intellectual, perceptual, informational, and environmental. [A] singular

> reference is inadequate when designing software for complex problem
> solving. (p. 15)

Although computer interfaces are a constant theme throughout this book, the issue is much larger: Interfaces are cultural constructions responding to, engendering, and being constantly modified by numerous, often contradictory, cultural forces.

Our cultures' relationships to technology, then, are much more complicated than they are normally portrayed. Any technology is much more than the sum of its constituent mechanical parts. Technologies are taken up and, functionally speaking, reconstructed by users within specific contexts. Numerous forces come together within that moment of use to structure and determine the specific nature of uses: Technology uses are articulations involving not simply isolated devices, but also specific users and contexts, political concerns, and whole technical systems. We see obvious continuity from one situation to the next, but we also see discontinuities when technologies are adapted in novel ways, when a new technology departs from earlier, similar technologies, when a social situation shifts, or when new users with different aptitudes and experiences take up a technology designed for a different type of user.

This emphasis on contingent articulations will take us through a wide range of situations, technologies, and users. We look at how IM programs crop up within classrooms and how they are involved in shifts in structures of learning and work. We examine the history of interface design to see the ways that different structures for representing information on a computer screen encourage or discourage different ways of working, thinking, and learning. We look at how how creativity changes in an information economy and how different physical environments for work empower or restrict the scope of creativity. Finally, we examine new approaches to learning and training that are aimed at living and working in information-saturated environments.

Here we go.

Notes

1. By *we* I mean people in the United States born after 1982—the year that I graduated from high school and the birth year for students entering Clarkson University the year I joined the faculty there and began the primary work on *Datacloud*. This date may be a coincidence, but I suspect otherwise.

2. The bug here obviously points to the metaphorical *bug* in software—a term derived from Grace Hopper's early discovery of a dead moth in a mainframe computer that was causing a malfunction.

3. Not that dystopic visions of the workplace have faded (see e.g., Mike Judge's *Office Space* (Rappaport, Rotenberg, & Judge, 1999—advertising images that feature a figure wrapped in Post-Its, carrying a briefcase, reminiscent of Harry Tuttle's demise in *Brazil*).

4. I return to Hall's work on articulation in chapter 2, where I lay out a framework for understanding the cultural situations involved in emerging ways of working and communicating in the datacloud.

5. These suggestions are something that computer theorists refer to as *affordances* (e.g., Norman, 1988): A computer mouse, for example, affords a different, broader range of cursor motion than the up/down/left/right arrow keys on keyboard. Technology theorist Feenberg (1997) distinguished *substantive* (completely out of a user's control) and *instrumental* (completely under a user's control) from *ambivalent* theories of technology. Ambivalent technologies may have inherent qualities that suggest specific uses, but those uses may be resisted/redirected, but not freely.

2

TENDENTIAL FORCES: A BRIEF PRIMER ON ARTICULATION THEORY AND SYMBOLIC-ANALYTIC WORK

With and through articulation, we engage the concrete in order to change it, that is, to rearticulate it. To understand theory and method in this way shifts perspective from the acquisition or application of an epistemology to the creative process of articulating, of thinking relations and connections as how we come to know and creating what we know. Articulation is, then, not just a thing (not just a connection) but a process of creating connections, much in the same way that hegemony is not domination but the process of creating and maintaining consensus or of co-ordinating interests.
—Slack (1996, p. 114)

[Articulation transforms] cultural studies from a model of communication (production-text-consumption; encoding-decoding) to a theory of contexts.
—Grossberg (1993, p. 4)

 [R]eality must be simplified so that it can be understood and manipulated in new ways. The symbolic analyst wields equations, formulae, analogies, models, constructs categories and metaphors in order to create possibilities for reinterpreting, and then rearranging, the chaos of data that are already swirling around us.
—R. Reich (1991, p. 229)

When I watch students in my classes dividing their attention between face-to-face class discussion and instant messenger (IM) conversations with friends outside of the classroom, part of me wants to pull the plug, march the class out of the computer lab we usually call home, and seek out a *real*

classroom, dammit, one with chairs and desks that we can arrange in a circle and just, you know, *talk to each other without distractions*, like we used
to when I was a TA. This all makes me feel so freaking *old*.

I'm getting over it.

Most of us are used to seeing fragmentation, in general, as a bad
thing. Breakdowns are negative; entropy, although unavoidable, must be
resisted. We build, we structure, we connect, we synthesize. We avoid
breaking things. Postmodernism is often constructed as a cultural threat, a
tempting but ultimately debilitating practice.

Yet what if breakdown is a necessary condition of our culture? What
happens if we accept Derrida's contention that context is never completely recoverable—that communication occurs not in the transfer of unified
bits from sender to receiver, but within the gaps in the slippages among
conversants? In other words (always *other words*), what if we begin to
understand communication as not an attempt to overcome noise in the
transmission of signal, but as the ongoing process of both breakdown and
reconstruction?

> You're walking. And you don't always realize it, but you're always
> falling. With each step you fall forward slightly. And then catch yourself
> from falling. Over and over, you're falling. And then catching yourself
> from falling. And this is how you can be walking and falling at the same
> time. (Anderson, 1982, n.p.)

In this chapter, I attempt to frame a way to understand this ongoing
breakdown and construction by linking what cultural studies theorists term
the process of articulation with the labor theory definition of symbolic-analytic work. Conceptual cross-pollination between the two areas provides
each with important aspects: Articulation describes the ideological formation of working symbolic-analytic subjects or, to put it another way, articulation deals with the ideological, whereas symbolic-analytic work deals
with the material.[1]

One persistent issue in this book—and in the world—is that symbolic-analytic workers tend toward conservative political viewpoints and upper
class status. I do not subscribe, however, to the vulgar marxist view that
class determines subject position. So in one sense, *Datacloud* is an attempt
to provide a broader group of participants with the ability to engage in symbolic-analytic work, colonizing the upper classes. The unions of symbolic-
analytic work and articulation, as I discuss later, also provides methods for
jamming the existing cultural system in interesting and powerful ways.

ARTICULATION THEORY

"Postmodernism" is the biggest success story going. And since it is, in essence, such a devastating story—precisely about American culture, it seems a funny thing to be so popular. It's like asking, how long can you live with the end of the world, how much of a bang can you get out of the big bang? And yet, apart from that, one has to come to terms with it.
—Stuart Hall (cited in Grossberg, 1996, p. 131)

I'm Feeling Lucky

—Google Search Option < http://www.google.com/ >

Hall intentionally provides a gateway into *articulation*—a theory and method he helped develop and extend over the last several decades. Hall's version of articulation builds on the work of several key social theorists, which Hall brings together—articulates—to construct a workable social theory for postmodernist cultures. Working with trajectories from Gramsci, Althusser, Foucault, Laclau, and others,[2] Hall constructs a neomarxist theory of cultural production that understands class as well as postmodernism, without sliding completely in one or the other. Subjects are constructed in cultural contexts, including class belongingness, but not without some ability to intervene in that construction. Although people are routinely constructed as ideological subjects without their noticing it, networks of social forces are never completely tied up; there are always little border skirmishes, forces pushing in opposing directions. Particularly in a postmodernist culture, subjectivities are multiple and often conflicting: Every parent is also a child; every seller is also a buyer; every yes is also a no.[3] Although we do not frequently pay attention to these ongoing ideological conflicts, they are always present. Ideologies are structured like languages, always open to shifting in the ways that words shift from context to context and over time. Like language, words cannot be redefined arbitrarily (particularly in larger communities).

This ongoing process of disarticulation and rearticulation provides two crucial aspects to understanding (and living within) contemporary culture:

1. Things—objects, words, actions, subjectivities, and so on—do not have timeless, anchored meanings.
2. However, things—objects, words, actions, subjectivities, and so on—do have meanings in practice because participants actively construct those meanings over and over again.

This dual nature—breakdown and construction—provides a tentative answer to the problem of postmodernism: The breakdown of subjectivities in postmodernism is not a problem to be solved or papered over, but merely one half of the process of meaning. As Hall said, postmodernism tended to posit the idea that there was **no necessary** *correspondence* between word and meaning or class and subjectivity. This notion was somehow shifted, almost unwittingly, to be the idea that there was *necessarily* **no correspondence**, which makes meaning impossible. Hall reminded us, then, that *no necessary correspondence* also means *no necessary noncorrespondence*: correspondences are possible, but they are contingent and must be actively constructed.

So how do these meanings correspond to objects, words, actions, subjectivities, and so on? Only in specific contexts and only because people participating in those contexts provide meanings in practice. As Slack (1996) explained it,

> Articulation is, then, not just a thing (not just a connection) but a process of creating connections, much in the same way that hegemony is not domination but the process of creating and maintaining consensus or of co-ordinating interests. (p. 114)

I use the term *conceptual objects* to stand in for a whole constellation of issues: objects, words, actions, systems, and so on. On the one hand, the substitution is simple shorthand; on the other hand, the term gets at a crucial idea: objects, words, actions, and so on (including meanings) exist meaningfully only within specific, contingent, dynamic contexts. Communities and users make meanings and uses, borrowing from history, from other communities with which they share members (including across media and linguistically shared spaces beyond the physical communities, places such as online forums and other shared media). We agree on meaningfulness in moments of arbitrary closure. In other words, conceptual objects are meaningful only in their relation to other conceptual objects. Articulations, as conceptual objects, exist uneasily at the confluence of networks of other associated conceptual objects.

To take a simple example, in the United States, the meaning of the political conceptual object "Democrat" exists most popularly in opposition to another associated conceptual object, "Republican." Although we would be hard put to identify exactly what each meant, we also commonly recognize that each tends to have certain types of meanings associated with it: Democrats, the story goes, are in favor of taxes to support social programs such as welfare and Medicaid, whereas Republicans are against the same social programs.

The incomplete closure of those terms, however, provides options for resisting those particular meanings. For example, during the 1990s, Republicans began rearticulating the term *Republican* in strategic ways to remove what they perceived as negative connotations to their opposition to social programs sponsored by Democrats. Social programs, they argued, should not be supported by taxes or government, but instead by charitable organizations such as churches or other community groups. This shift (which is still the site of struggle over meanings) involved more than a simple decision to change the meaning of the term *Republican*. The project of rearticulating that aspect of what *Republican* meant involved a coordinated set of actions, communications, meetings, publications, and more. Some of these activities were formally planned in Republican National Committee forums and meetings or other official spaces; others took place in discussions at schools, workplaces, homes, online, and in the media.

At the same time, Democrats initiated an associated set of efforts that resisted this rearticulation, attempting to shore up the earlier set of meanings through a similar loose constellation of official and unofficial activities. Debates among the groups occurred in the media, in governmental meetings, in communities, and more. Legislation was introduced, argued over, revised, passed and rejected. Participants in social programs, both traditional governmental and those sponsored by community or religious organizations, both clients and staff, administrators and volunteers, all engaged in various forms of debate, struggling in the processes of rearticulation.

We would all agree that the meaning of the two terms has shifted, perhaps slightly, in relation to this complex set of ongoing and contingent processes. These processes illustrate several key aspects of articulation.

First, conceptual objects—articulations—are contingent and open to change. Second, change involves struggle among competing forces. Changing the meaning of a conceptual object is not just a decision to be made or a proposal to be voted on. Third, conceptual objects, as articulations, are never separate from the forces that construct them: Articulations are formed through the differential sets of other articulations. Fourth, different concrete contexts necessarily construct articulations that vary in different aspects and degrees, so that, for example, *social program* continues to generally mean one type of thing to Republicans and another to Democrats because slightly different social forces push on that articulation in different contexts. Fifth, fragmentation and rupture are not necessarily debilitating. Indeed the inherent contingency and possibility of fragmentation requires socially active participants who are able to work for both stability and change. What is remarkable about this process is that meanings are possible at all.

SYMBOLIC-ANALYTIC WORK[4]

Symbolic-analytic workers inhabit a job classification created by R. Reich (1991), primarily in *The Work of Nations* (and later extended in *The Future of Success*). In this text, Reich was primarily interested in analyzing shifts in the nature of service work in the U.S. economy (he was the U.S. Secretary of Labor at that time). As Reich illustrated, the service worker economy was shifting away from the production of industrial objects (and in some cases, the management of those workers as well) and toward face-to-face or in-person service: those who complete routine, relatively undervalued tasks for people they encounter in person (e.g., clerical workers, food-service workers, etc.). So although the U.S. economy continued to engage in industrial production—and will for quite some time—service work is becoming the primary area of new jobs.

At the same time, Reich noted the emergence of a new type of service worker: the symbolic-analytic worker. Although some workers within this classification hold traditional titles, Reich mapped the value of these workers across occupational boundaries. In addition, he lent emphasis to the idea that, in a postindustrial age, the most valued workers no longer produce concrete objects, but conceptual objects.

People in this type of work identify, rearrange, circulate, abstract, and broker information in response to specific, concrete situations. They work with information and symbols to produce reports, plans, and proposals. They also tend to work online, either communicating with peers (they rarely have direct organizational supervision) or manipulating symbols. Their job titles including investment banker, research scientist, lawyer, management consultant, strategic planner, and architect. Finally, as Reich later modified the idea (2001), the most valued symbolic-analytic workers possess qualities of both "geek" (technical expert) and "shrink" (psychologist). Symbolic-analytic workers have much in common with Speilberg's detective in *Minority Report*, collecting, rearranging, filtering, and connecting bits of information for particular contexts and needs.

As I said previously, we might think of symbolic-analytic workers as technical rhetoricians or rhetorical technologists. This formulation provides a wedge for opening up the common tendency for symbolic-analytic work to an ethical stance missing from much of Reich's work.

Symbolic-analytic workers possess the abilities to identify, rearrange, circulate, abstract, and broker information. Their principle work materials are information and symbols, and their principle products are reports, plans, and proposals. They frequently work online, either communicating with peers (they rarely have direct organizational supervision) or manipulating symbols with the help of various computer resources. Symbolic analysts go by a wide variety of job titles, including investment banker, research scientist, lawyer, management consultant, strategic planner, and architect.

In most ways, symbolic analysts differ from the other job classifications in terms of status, responsibility, geographic mobility, and pay. Unlike routine production workers, they are more able to move from place to place because of their higher disposable incomes and because companies will often pay moving expenses for their services. They can also frequently telecommute, uploading and downloading information over the World Wide Web, Internet, and intranets; faxing reports to clients; and conference calling on the telephone or Internet. Unlike in-person service workers (who may communicate with customers via phone, fax, or computer network as well as face to face), symbolic-analytic workers deal with situations not easily addressed by routine solutions.

Reich outlined four key areas of education for symbolic analysts that we can use to reinvent education in a postindustrial age: collaboration, experimentation, abstraction, and system thinking.

Experimentation involves forming and testing hypotheses about information and communication. For symbolic analysts, this experimentation is sometimes formally scientific, but also sometimes intuitive. Because of the unique nature of most work done by symbolic analysts, preconceived approaches are, at best, only starting points. If a class of problems becomes so common that it can be answered by reference to a rulebook, the problem moves into the domain of routine production work.

Collaboration helps symbolic analysts work together to solve problems while crossing complex disciplinary domains. Software projects, for example, typically require not only programmers, but user interface designers, marketing experts, usability testers, technical communicators, and graphic artists. Team members brainstorm ideas and solutions, critique each other's work, and provide support and feedback to the team mates.

Abstraction requires people to learn to discern patterns, relationships, and hierarchies in large masses of information.

As with other aspects of symbolic-analytic work, the low profile of abstraction as a skill relates partially to notions of authorship that prioritize the creation of original content and subordinate work that seems derivative and functional.[5] As cultural theorist Lyotard (1984) among others has argued, traditional originality in a postmodern era is of declining value or, at the very least, traditional originality now competes with a postmodern sense of creativity as symbolic-analytic work. Market analysts locate and rearrange information in massive data warehouses to create projections and scenarios to guide strategic planning; turntablists manipulate the playback of vinyl albums on turntables—scratching, reversing, transforming—to create a new sound from the fragments of the old.[6]

System thinking works at a level above abstraction, requiring symbolic analysts to recognize and construct relationships and connections in extremely broad, often apparently unrelated domains. Systems thinking works *beyond* problem-solving approaches to understand (and remake) systemic conditions. In other words, whereas traditional approaches to problem solving tend to rely heavily on breaking a problem into small, manageable parts to be solved by short, simple help texts, a symbolic analyst would step back to look at larger issues in the system to determine how the problem develops and in what contexts it is considered a problem.

Because of the complexity and broad reach of system thinking, this skill has proved extremely difficult to carry over into practice—such concerns are external to models that prioritize technology over communication and learning. In fact advocates of minimalist documentation (e.g., Caroll, 1990) argued that computer documentation should abandon the attempt to provide broad, conceptual materials for users. Yet such a position, although it may certainly increase accuracy and speed in the short term, disempowers users by assuming as a rule that they already know how to complete their general tasks (writing a memo, composing a presentation, etc.). Furthermore, the decontexualized, functionalist position prevents consideration of sociopolitical terms. A model of communication that presents technology as neutral and discrete makes invisible the social reproduction of gender bias inherent in technological development and use. As I suggested earlier, articulation theory offers one way to pry open this functionalist perspective.

REARTICULATING WORKING AND LEARNING

As I mentioned earlier, the increasing use of IM programs is only one of many places in which working and learning are being rearticulated in our culture, reforming along what philosophers and literary theorists would call *postmodern lines*. In nearly every aspect of contemporary life, our activities are increasingly infiltrated with these new types of working and learning— of living. I sometimes hesitate to continue to use the terms *contamination* or *breakdown* to describe these trends because they put too negative a spin on the phenomenon. In many ways, these shifts are potentially positive cultural trends even if we often fail to recognize them as such. In fact we often rail against the new forms because they threaten our traditional ways of living: We condemn computer users for not having a real life, we dismiss new processes for working as chaotic, and we chide our children for not paying attention. We fail to understand that these new structures and processes are not merely breakdowns or failure, although breakdown and failure are, interestingly, often functional and important aspects of such work. These new structures and processes often hold within them the potential to remake our worlds in positive and exciting ways. That remaking, that rearticulation, seems inevitable; we need to decide whether we want to use the opportunity to participate in that remaking or if we want to flail helplessly in its midst.

Throughout this book, I attempt to frame some of the potentially positive features in these rearticulated structures and processes, ranging from computer games and education through video and music production and Web site design. I highlight key features of these developments, suggesting ways that we can both assist in their potentially positive aspects as well as apply those aspects as tendential forces to other activities and objects, often far afield from their origins. Origins are always suspect; inventors never work in isolation, but always bring with them experiences from diverse and scattered domains.

Tangled inextricably with the shift toward new forms of working and learning, we find, as you might expect, people using computers in ways both new and old. I want to avoid the assertion that computers are the general cause of these shifts, but they are certainly associated with those shifts and provide some of the starkest examples. We might position such forms of working and learning as a symptom of postmodern capitalism as described by Jameson (1991) or the new order of science as described by Lyotard (1984)—both of whose analyses implicitly if not explicitly affirm analyses and predictions by business and labor theorists including R. Reich (1991, 2001) and Drucker (1988), among others. Briefly put, much recent theory and practice in management, corporate communication, and marketing centers on the ability of decentered, structurally flat organizations to respond dynamically to shifting market conditions and technical situations. Workers in such corporations, like the students in my classes, rely heavily on their abilities to communicate rapidly and in multiple media, to organize and circulate information, and to attack problems in creative, nontraditional ways. Increasingly, users in such spaces—both microcontexts and macrocontexts—work and learn within visually and structurally dense, often frankly and intentionally chaotic spaces. They multitask, they surf, they filter and rearrange, and they push and pull data streams. The often-held separation between online and IRL ("In Real Life") is fairly tenuous, with relationships developed online spilling over into the real world; information at the surface or at depth in the computer moves back and forth to PDA, web-enabled phone, video monitor, stereo, and more.

In the rest of this book, I examine the ways that new forms of working, communicating, and living are emerging in several social contexts. By analyzing the social and technological forces that construct each of these particular instances, we can gain a better understanding of how people work within diverse types of technical and social situations.

Notes

1. This is not to say that each of these theories does not already refer to both ideological and material aspects. *Cultural studies* in general focuses on how people engage with concrete aspects of the material world in an ongoing, ideological constructive process, whereas *symbolic-analytic* work inherently requires specific ideological positionings of workers in global economies. I combine the two terms here to bring these productive tensions to the surface.
2. Useful orientations to the work informing Hall's version of articulation can be found in Grossberg and Slack (1985) and Hall (1983, 1985, 1989). Morley's (1986) edited collection on Hall's work (including many reprints of Hall's work) also offers an extensive array of resources.
3. Not in the Orwellian sense, but in the sense that saying "yes" to one option requires saying "no" to others—choosing one way of using a technology implies discarding others.
4. Some material in this section has been adapted from Johnson-Eilola (1997).
5. Foucault (1977) discussed the ways that current notions of authorship prioritize certain practices while subordinating or even rejecting others in "What is an Author?"
6. A later chapter deals with turntablism in much greater detail.

3

TOWARD FLATNESS: CHANGING ARTICULATIONS OF INTERFACE DESIGN

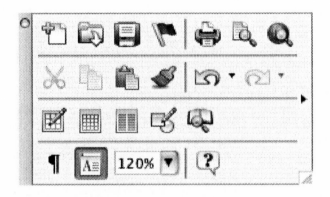

—Palette in Microsoft Word v.X for the Macintosh

I am almost embarrassed to suggest that the majority of this chapter attempts to make a big deal out of this commonsense observation: How we use computers has changed dramatically in the last 50 years. Yet examining the changing ways that computers—and, in this case, interfaces—have been articulated sheds much light on how we relate to computers today. In addition, changes occurring in interface design over the last several decades highlight the rise of symbolic-analytic work because several of these changes reflect efforts to better support these forms of work. Another category of changes in interface explicitly supports in-person service work. I return to this issue later because it illustrates the ways in which job classifications are frequently drawn along gendered lines without regard to job skills.

In this history, we look not only at the technical aspects of the inter-face, such as the layout of information on the screen and the ways that bits of information are connected together. We also look at the ways that com-puters become integrated in work through evolving processes and struc-tures for learning, professionalizing jobs, developing educational frame-works, and forming communities.

In analyzing these continued processes of articulation and rearticula-tion, we begin to see a recursive development in which the computer absorbs social actions, fragments and flattens them, only to have those actions and spaces reabsorbed into culture in various ways. However, I want to avoid the idea that the computer interface somehow autonomous-ly *causes* broad social changes. Instead I want to suggest that the comput-er *participates* in broad social changes. In a recursive and contingent process (or set of processes), particular forms of interface tend to influence how people work. At the same time, existing institutional structures also influence the forms and processes of work within and without those inter-faces. To this continual rearticulation, we would add social forces such as colleagues, supervisors, subordinates, and other social actors as well as the whole experiential history of the acting person within the space. Even advertisements and other forms of media—including film—exert strong tendential forces on the development of computer interfaces.[1] In short, particular forms of interface that I discuss here do not appear out of nowhere: They are typically afforded in particular contexts precisely because they provide added force to one or more strands that already artic-ulate work in that location. In some instances, the tendential forces already co-exist in particular situations and recursively reinforce each other. The development of a program like VisiCalc for personal computers (Fig. 3.1), an early spreadsheet program that convinced many small business owners to purchase their first personal computer, brought together several tenden-tial forces: the common use of the computer as a calculating device, the availability of relatively inexpensive computer technologies (compared with the cost of computers in the 1960s) driven in parallel by the need for growth by large computer corporations, the demand for complex formulae and easy recalculations in small businesses, and even tax laws relating to capital equipment investment, and more all contributed to the growth of the computer as an office technology.

In other instances, tendential forces are brought together in conscious efforts to change particular articulations: Rapid changes in intellectual property law over the last several decades are ongoing rearticulations of intellectual property regulations developed during a several 100-year histo-ry, the specific articulations of which are now being aggressively battled over. For example, one camp attempts to strengthen the existing articulation of "idea" as "real property," whereas the other camp challenges that articulation and argues that "idea" is either "community property" or "freedom of speech" (and not property at all). Both sides bring in external tendential forces in the form of logical arguments, connotations, market analyses (with figures for "lost value"), and so on. In all of these cases, there are no simple, detached, neutral technologies or concepts, but ongoing, contingent, and often contentious sites of struggle.

Fig. 3.1. VisiCalc, early Apple II spreadsheet program. © Dan Bricklin (Used with permission).

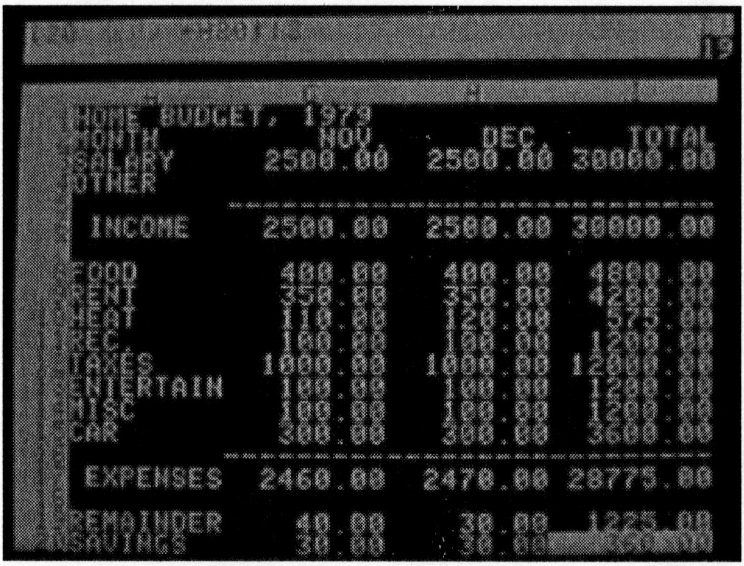

Current theories of understanding computer use suggest movement toward either virtual realities or ubiquitous computing contexts.[2] In actuality, however, we seem headed toward an environment in which the distinction between the two is meaningless: Work and learning both happen within and across information contexts, online, and face to face.

In this chapter, I sketch a rough history of computers as technologies for work. In each era of that history, I focus on two aspects of how the computer is constructed and used. First, I examine the microcontext of user work and learning—that is, the location of information about learning to work with the computer. Second, I consider the social and political implications of those different spatial constructions, connecting up specific shapes and processes of work to historical and developing trends in labor, economics, and politics.

A BRIEF HISTORY OF COMPUTER INTERFACES

In this history, I am not concerned with specific dates or technologies, only general trends. Later in this chapter I attempt to situate several specific interfaces and uses within this framework to examine how those concrete articulations are constructed (and how they might be challenged). This rough history provides a network of broad tendential forces—such as workplace genres and technology configurations—that both perpetuate and influence specific articulations. Table 3.1 begins to open up this network, providing a way to view successive technological developments that are caught up in (mutually constructed by and constructing) other trends, such as workforce training and work habits in the shift from industrial to information economies.

Hardwired: Interface as a Simple Tool

Historically, an interface was the physical connection of two devices, an articulation in the strictest sense of the word—a hardware register interfacing with an output device such as a teletype. Computers, at the earliest stages, were programmed by rewiring them.

The key aspect here for our discussion is the location of knowledge about how to use the computer. With these early computer, users learned to program and work with the computers through apprentice-type relations: Users worked with an expert who, over time, taught them functional skills.

The photo of Eniac being programmed by Ester Gurston and Gloria Gordon (Fig. 3.2) is of interest not merely because it illustrates the mechanical nature of early computer programming, but also because the image is of two women programmers in an industry that, at least recently, has been dominated by men. There are numerous examples of influential women early in the history of computing—from Ada Lovelace to Grace Hopper. Yet as computer programming and engineering became professions, they were most frequently articulated as male positions. As in most articulations, it would be deceptive to posit a cause-and-effect relationship or conscious program of discrimination (although there certainly were—and are—com-

Table 3.1: Models of Interface

INTERFACE	LOCATION OF WORK AND LEARNING	POLITICAL AND ECONOMIC CONTEXT
Hardwired	Outside interface: education, training (few manuals)	Cold war era; industrial economy
Punch cards	Outside interface: education, training, manuals, courses	Cold war era; industrial economy; rise of white-collar work
Command-line interface	Outside interface or at second-level deep in interface: education, training, manuals, courses, man pages	Industrial economy in decline; cold war in decline; information work rising
Graphical interface	Into interface: shifting toward *limited* interface (surface)	Move toward information economy; self-directed office work (white collar, clerical) and development of flattened hierarchy, TQM, etc. in industry
Spatial online (beginnings of the datacloud)	Interface expands beyond physical boundaries to allow social (online) communication	dot.com boom; rise of knowledge worker in information economy; industrial sector shrinking
Spatial/hybrid, information-saturated workspaces	Boundaries of interface break apart to support movement (including arrangement, eddies and flows) not only social/online, but also local microcontext	dot.com bubble bursts; economic slide; information work infiltrates nearly every sector of workplace (office and industrial)

Fig. 3.2. Ester Gerston and Gloria Gordon (left to right) programming Eniac (U.S. Army photo). < http://ftp.arl.mil.ftp/historic-computers/ >

mon and widespread examples of women being discouraged from entering computer programming). However, we can also recognize that the articulation of computer programmer includes the historical tendential force that fills high-status occupations with male subjects.

Clerical work, to offer a similarly gendered example working in the opposite direction, was initially a male-dominated profession. As clerical work became routinized and deskilled, the positions tended to be articulated as female (Zuboff, 1989). Similarly, the relatively low status given to clerical work ignores that, although much clerical work can be characterized as routine and low skilled, there exist numerous examples of clerical positions that require extremely high symbolic-analytic skills. The common joke about specific clerical workers "really running things around here"—usually a highly skilled woman coordinating the work of a higher paid but less skilled male manager—often contains more than a grain of truth and bitter irony.

In the early articulation of computer programming, the interface to the computer joins two otherwise separate objects—wires or switches.[3] In a real sense, these first interfaces focused not on the user and computer, but on the transmission of electrical impulses between two separate elements of the computer. The computer existed primarily as an automating device. As such the focus of work with a computer was much larger than the computer: The mapping out and specification of calculations to perform, problems to solve, and so on occurred outside of the computer. Only after the problem was decomposed into sets of relatively straightforward calculations was the computer included.

More important, that knowledge and use were also more powerfully and explicitly embedded in real social contexts. At least partially due to the highly specialized nature of early computers, learning to use a computer was something one learned by apprenticeship, collaboration, or by being an inventor of the technology. The apparatus required for more traditional forms of learning—textbooks, courses—required a relatively large economy of scale that was not present in these early days.

As we begin to move toward other models for information/work space, we begin to notice some slow, but profound, changes in the shape of those spaces.

I am being nostalgic about apprenticeships here, obviously—I am not calling for a return to this situation, but instead a reflection on how this articulation relates to other situations. The apprenticeship model presupposes a particular economic and industrial process—one that values in-depth, long-term investments in workers, particularly in professions that value craft. At this stage, the computer is not a mass-production, mass-market device, but rather a specialized, vertical tool. In addition, although computers were information-processing devices, computing was not considered information work in the current sense. Rather, computers solved complex, but predictable, problems such as weapon trajectories.

As we trace the changing shape of the computer interface, we see that computer use shifted from a structure of *depth* to one of *surface*. In this early articulation, computer use required the ability to manipulate the configuration of the physical artifact. Similarly, learning to use the computer was a temporal process, often largely invisible, portioned out bit by bit in interactions between expert and apprentice (Fig. 3.3).

As we look at later rearticulations, we see that as computer use came to focus more on surface-level display of information, learning to use the computer became less temporal.

Computer as Complex Object

Whereas initial computer technologies were used almost completely as discrete artifacts, two parallel developments led to different working and learn-

Fig. 3.3. Trends in interface articulation.

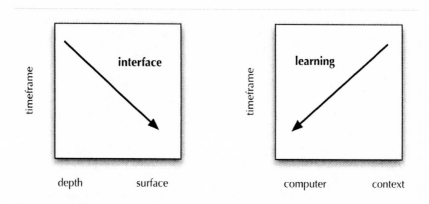

ing microcontexts. The size of a computer began to shrink while processing speed and complexity increased dramatically, allowing a more mutable and powerful type of work to be done with the computer. This development spurred wider adoption and relative standardization of both hardware and software, including the development of batch and interactive processing.

In this gradual rearticulation, the workspace of the computer expands to include more complex tasks such as modeling, finance, and other mathematically focused work. Still the space of the computer tended to support relatively small-scale, but computationally intensive activities. Although the complexity and fluidity of operations available increased dramatically with the possibility of batch processing, actually *using* the computer was normally a brief segment of the work routine. Programs were often planned out first on paper with flowcharts, converted tediously to handwritten code for debugging and examination, followed by painstaking translation to an intermediary medium such as punch cards (Fig. 3.4). Cards would be stacked and carried to the operations room, where, after standing in line, the user would hand over a stack of cards to an operator who would place them into a hopper for loading into the queue, where patterns of holes punched into each individual card would be again translated into data to run in batches. Output would be delivered to a printer where the user could pick it up.

Obviously, this articulation of the interface is similar to the earlier hardwired interface in that little user work goes on within the interface. Most of the process of working (the breakdown of a problem into an algorithm, the translation of the algorithm into routines or modules, the coding

**Fig. 3.4. Punchcard from *The WWW Virtual Punchcard (Punch Card)
Server* < http://facade.com/legacy/punchcard/ >
(Katz, n.d./2004).**

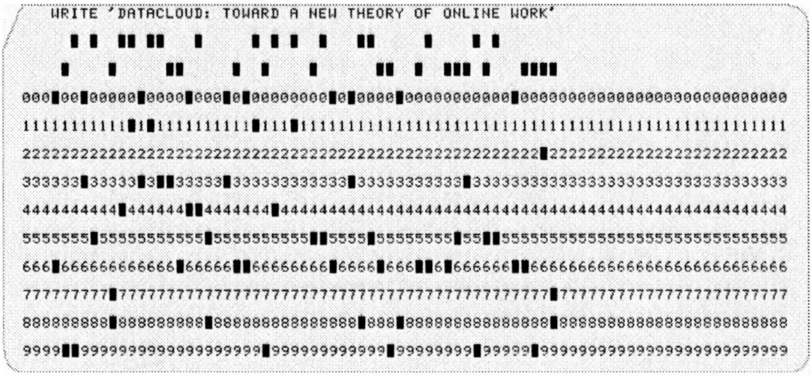

of the program data) takes place in other areas. The work that does occur at the interface involves configuring the device (loading programs, etc.) and then running a batch operation—tasks often not completed by the user, but by a systems operator. The majority of intellectual work continues to take place outside the computer and away from the interface.

Yet whereas apprenticeship or craftwork marked the earlier articulation, the increasing use of the computer in various settings (corporations and universities primarily) provided force to the rearticulation of the computer as a device used by many groups of people rather than a single person. Although the complexity of mainframe computers grew to support increasingly complex (and varied) types of programs, the need for more systematic, enterprise-wide (or school-wide) training also increased.

Rearticulations frequently represent a chicken-and-egg problem: Which came first? Symbolic-analytic workers or interfaces and social contexts to support them?

Neither. Each emerged slowly, contingently, gathering force from the other (as well as mutually reinforcing forces). As the industrial age declined and the information economy rose, demand for more complex forms of information work developed. This development was fueled by numerous forces—changing market economies, NAFTA, increased international trade, transnational capitalism, advertising, and more, including, to some extent, the development of interfaces and social networks (educational, political, economic) that supported symbolic-analytic work. At the same time, symbolic-analytic work contributed in substantial ways to many of those same forces. In a recursive way, articulations connect up to other articulations and lend weight to corresponding tendential forces in complex, contingent, and noncausal ways.

Within the microcontext of work and learning, the standardization allowed the development of nonapprentice learning, first with the development of software and hardware manuals and then with technology training courses. In a sense, the adoption of print-based training materials acts as a contraction of the social context of learning and working, with new users separated from existing users.

Likewise, the economics of textbooks and manuals require a mass market, one in which education is discrete, repeatable, and marketable, with student customers who are willing to pay (or have their employers pay) for education from which they might profit later.

These rearticulations also provide the beginning of the development of a context—of systems, professional communities, and flexible tools—that afford symbolic-analytic work. This development is neither coincidental nor completely intentional, but mutually constructing in an evolutionary sense.[4]

Peering Into the Black Box: Interface as Portal

Additional (and apparently perpetual) increases in the complexity and available storage space of computers are associated with an additional contraction of the microcontext of learning and work: Information about how to use the computer becomes integrated into the computer. This development is a gradual one and not apparent at first glance. Figure 3.2 shows a contemporary command-line interface nearly identical to the buried information model of this phase.

When I said that some knowledge about using the computer became embedded in the computer, I did not mean that using the computer suddenly became obvious. For example, on my linux server, the command prompt "johndan@localhost johndan" offers precious little information about how to use the system. Yet if I know enough about how linux (or a closely related OS) operates, I know I can type in *man* (user's *manual*) on page command to get help on system commands. From an expert user's standpoint, this is great because if a user has a general working knowledge of how the operating system works, they can bootstrap that knowledge by reading online help.[5] However, the user has to know (a) what the man command is, and (b) the name of a command to connect up to—in this case, the "chmod" command (Figs. 3.5 and 3.6).

Fig. 3.5. Command-line interface.

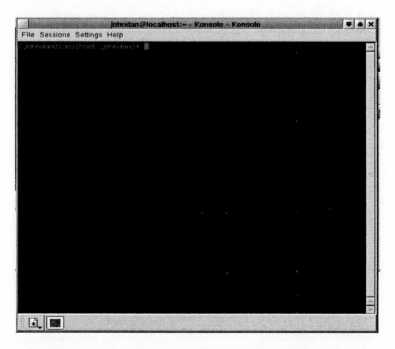

Gaining this background knowledge typically meant doing something outside the computer interface—taking a course, working with another expert user, buying a book, and so on. New types of microcontext do not completely erase previous ones—people continue to work in apprenticeship systems and use print manuals today. The history I am constructing here is an uneven one with numerous overlaps. Indeed, the deep-information model probably also requires the existence of earlier models to acculturate, at the very least, novices who need assistance getting to the point where they can use the deep information.

The deep-information model serves as a marker of market maturation in a sense—the size of the market for learning how to operate this particular type of computer is robust enough to support not only apprentice-based learning, but a growing variety of learning types. Whereas instruction of single, isolated novices might be feasible via face-to-face apprentice work, larger populations of distributed novices are often easier to educate using standardized materials.

Fig. 3.6. Online help in Linus man page.

The computer interface also becomes a context supporting symbolic-analytic work in important if still limited ways: The increasing ease with which symbols could be entered, transformed, rearranged, and transmitted affords a different order of work than a hard-wired computing system. Whereas previously intellectual labor with the computer involved only a small (but critical) portion of work (specific number-intensive calculations), rewriting electronic memory registers coupled with the capability for offline storage (punchcards, tapes, etc.) meant that massive amounts of information could not only be stored and calculated, but also searched, rearranged, filtered, transmitted, and combined with other datasets.

The microcontext of deep help systems affords a particular type of learning for particular types of users. The structure of the man page, for example, is oriented around concrete, functional uses: A one-line definition of the command followed by a synopsis of command syntax possibilities is at the top, allowing users to drop from the command line (surface) to the slightly deep definition and synopsis. To browse more in-depth information, users are required to stay (at depth) for a significantly longer amount of time. Furthermore, linux man pages do not support (or at least obviously support) long-term, complex learning situations. Such long-term, complex learning takes place *somewhere*, but that learning is more likely scattered around the computer in notes and texts as well as distributed on the network with other users.

This rearticulation was gradual and partial rather than rapid and full. For example, early error messages (even in noninteractive systems) often contained troubleshooting data that directed users toward specific types of solutions (not always successful ones). The structure of the computer, especially early systems, clearly encouraged certain types of operations (e.g., calculation of large statistical operations) while discouraging others (word processing), although even those forces could be eroded provided enough force was applied.

Flattening Space: Interface as Surface

As we move toward more graphical interfaces, the location of working and learning information begins to shift; learning is buried in the interface (in online help and tutorials), but increasingly the interface—the surface—provides users with suggestions and hints about how to work. In other words, learning and work increasingly take place at the surface of the computer. The interface captures multiple, overlapping spaces that support an increasingly complex array of tasks: word processing, e-mail, graphics design, page layout, presentation design, video, and more (e.g., the analysis and manipulation of symbols).

In the screenshot shown in Fig. 3.7, users of the Web site design program Dreamweaver are given literally thousands of visual cues that suggest to them how to work, completely apart from any suggestions they may receive from their immediate social context or deep forms of help (online tutorials, print manuals, etc.).

As information about work moves to the surface, it becomes fragmented and flattened in ways that simultaneously support ease of use and discourage broad, complex forms of learning. Although traditionally such education has been dismissed as immature or surface level (pun intended), these types of learning are specifically demanded by some variations of just-in-time and project-based learning, among other areas. In a recursive loop, the success of such interfaces in those particular work situations increases the surfacing of information in subsequent versions of interface design.

Fig. 3.7. Surface information in Dreamweaver.

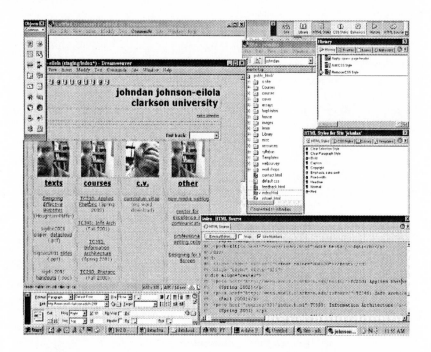

More important, although surfaced interfaces frequently cause learn-ing and usage problems for users in more traditional job functions, extremely information-dense interfaces are effective at supporting emerg-ing forms of work crucial to the rapidly growing information economy—particularly those that rely on the ability to experiment with and within complex and changing masses of information (a facility increasingly required in a range of jobs, from financial analysis to nonlinear audio/video production).

The screenshot of the Dreamweaver interface shows my work on the main page of my own Web site late last year. Although there is a great deal of learning support available for Dreamweaver (and Web design in gener-al)—in manuals, on the Web, in users' groups, and so on—most users build Web pages in Dreamweaver without referring to that outside work. Instead, based on their experiences of other computer programs and seeing other Web pages, they muddle through the procedure based on surfaced infor-mation: palettes that offer them a range of often-used commands; menus that, by their very names, suggest certain types of actions as more common than others; and windows containing information that can be acted and interacted with. In other words, the interface strongly suggests action and, through trial and error (play), they make their way.

On the one hand, surfaced information represents an opportunity— the ease of use here provides important cues that put an immense amount of design power in the hands of people who would not normally have that power. Although relatively speaking HTML codes are pretty straightforward, the knowledge about how to use those codes does prevent many novice users from creating Web sites. So this is, in one sense, a good thing—a democratization of technology. For example, my own home page contains JavaScript image rollovers that cause the four main images on the page to reverse themselves when a user's mouse hovers over each—a standard method for signalling potential interactivity. By convention, users expect this activity to signal that the images can be clicked like links (which is true in this instance); they also add visual activity to the page and server to mark me as a designer with some measure of technical expertise.[6] The function for creating a JavaScript rollover in Dreamweaver is contained, for the most part, in the palettes shown in this Fig. 3.8.

Fig. 3.8. Dreamweaver palettes controlling image rollover (lower right of window).

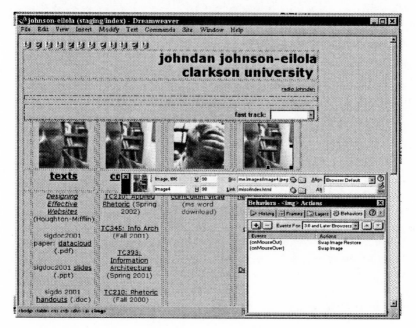

In traditional HTML, the process is relatively more complex (particularly to someone who does not understand HTML and JavaScript). The image is referenced in this bit of text:

```
<a href="misc/index.html"
onMouseOver="MM_swapImage('image4','','images/welcome.
images/image4.roll.jpeg',1)"
onMouseOut="MM_swapImgRestore()"><img
src="images/welcome.images/image4.jpeg" width="98"
height="98" border="0" name="image4"></a>
```

This code describes the endpoint of the link referenced, the location of the image file to be swapped in place of the existing image, and the original image. The code also calls two other program functions—one to swap the new image in for the old one (MM_swapImage):

```
function MM_swapImage() { //v3.0
   var i,j=0,x,a=MM_swapImage.arguments;
document.MM_sr=new Array; for(i=0;i<(a.length-2);i+=3)
   if
((x=MM_findObj(a[i]))!=null){document.MM_sr[j++]=x;
if(!x.oSrc) x.oSrc=x.src; x.src=a[i+2];}
```

and one to return the old image when the pointer leaves the area (MM_swapImageRestore):

```
function MM_swapImgRestore() { //v3.0
   var i,x,a=document.MM_sr;
for(i=0;a&&i<a.length&&(x=a[i])&&x.oSrc;i++)
x.src=x.oSrc;
}
```

I will be the first to admit that, although at one point in my work as a Web designer I understood how these commands worked, more or less, I now rely so heavily on Dreamweaver's surfaced information interface that I cannot verify that the code I have pasted in is either complete or accurate. Is this a problem? Not really.

There is little reason for most people to know technical details such as this. Although some technical expertise is crucial, I know from experience that it is more important that I know how to learn new technical skills on the fly as needed. They are needed much more rarely than most experts would lead you to believe. For example, I have not needed to debug

Javascript rollover code in 3 years despite frequently using this code in Dreamweaver during that time. Although I am not completely clueless about JavaScript, I see little need to code rollovers directly, and I see little need to force new users into JavaScript coding when the surfaced information in Dreamweaver will likely be as much as they need.

I routinely talk to coding experts who deride programs such as Dreamweaver, arguing that to *really* design a Web site designers have to subject themselves to the rigor of coding by hand. Although expert Web designers should be able to dissect a piece of code to debug broken tags or control elements with greater precision, insisting that designers work in the deep information environment exclusively (i.e., coding by hand) not only dismisses the importance of visual layout design, it seems like little more than an attempt by someone already holding power to prevent anyone else from entering that domain without extensive—if pointless—effort.

Paradoxically, increased ease of use also worries me; it is now much more likely that people will create Web pages without a broader learning context—without understanding anything about interactivity, screen layout, and information design. Note that this is quite apart from the technical coding issues discussed earlier because learning functional codes often takes place in the absence of conceptual discussions (in fact the people I know who insist most viciously on either code *or* layout views are those who lack much experience with the facet they subordinate). In a sense, the ease of use tends to move the task of constructing basic Web pages away from a symbolic-analytic skill and toward a routine production or in-person service skill. Indeed at my own university, the task of maintaining Web pages is frequently the domain of clerical workers, who are probably just as likely as anyone else on campus to possess the commonsense, problem-management skills, and dedication to learn the skills necessary, but who offered little in the way of technical training, much less effective conceptual education about Web site design. Even those who possess or learn more advanced Web design and maintenance skills are not frequently given the opportunity to demonstrate their abilities in ways valued by the university.

In subsequent versions of Dreamweaver, information about work is surfaced even more aggressively. Earlier versions, for example, provided separate windows for editing code by hand and for editing page layout directly in a graphical environment. In Dreamweaver MX, code and layout views inhabit the same window, allowing users to switch back and forth between views or (in the default setting) split the window to show layout in one portion and code in another (Fig. 3.9). Similar surfacing has taken place with online help, scripting, and other features.

Fig. 3.9. Increasingly surface information in Dreamweaver MX.

Yet what has happened in the surfacing of information in Dreamweaver is that only a small fraction of the learning was surfaced: There is only so much real estate on which information can be displayed. Although code is now commonly visible to users, there exists little scaffolding for understanding the relationships between that code and the visual layout. In general, this surface does provide a path toward increased learning about how code operates, but users will not likely follow that path without additional educational support.

More to the point, Dreamweaver (and other common office productivity programs) increasingly offer low-level functional help—technology training—but completely ignore concepts and broader forms of learning necessary for advanced education and work. In Dreamweaver, for example, the interface is beginning to include reference manuals (or at least links to them) at the surface level, which can provide important resources for learning. Yet key concepts such as layout principles or usability heuristics are absent. Web design is articulated as a primarily technical/functional skill for novice users.

That is not to say that Dreamweaver is not used for more sophisticated design. The program remains one of the leading applications used by professional Web site designers to construct elegant, complex, and useful sites. Yet these designers have learned basic design skills elsewhere—in courses, by experience, and through design conversations with other designers.

It would be disingenuous to blame this gap on Dreamweaver's designers: Convincing users to learn concepts and frameworks has long been more difficult than showing them simple functions. One can get by, albeit in a haphazard way, without theory, but it is difficult to get anywhere without function. In this instance, the tendential forces demanding productivity militate against broader forms of learning for many users. I know from experience that if a user can get by with what is present, they are less likely to go further. In fact trying to learn higher level skills is frequently seen as wasting company time, as dissatisfaction with one's stage in life. One manager in Zuboff's (1989) research on workplace automation study noted that if he saw one worker going to another's desk to ask questions, he would suspect that the first worker needed additional training.[7]

It's the Great Chain of Online Being: Hope No Higher.

Where previously work was enmeshed in a social context—and learning how to work involved a process of education over time—work now is increasingly fragmented and flattened. Learning how to work is shrunken and decontextualized so that only the most functional aspects are visible at the surface. In effect, the interface is not simply a tool, but a structure for work—a set of forces articulating a specific form of work, a set of forces articulating work.

The space of learning and work here has collapsed: Work is no longer something visibly, socially situated in a large space (an office, a classroom, etc.), but now has condensed, in many ways, into a 19-inch glass window. In addition, as that workspace has collapsed, it has sucked learning right down with it. However, because the pace of work has accelerated, the information space has flattened, with users increasingly unlikely to look outside their immediate interface for assistance on using the computer—assistance that used to frequently position the technical, functional aspects of their work within a broader, richer framework.

These contradictory tendential forces—the technological and managerial forces pushing users into the interface against the user's need to break out of the interface—lead to tensions expressed in nearly every contemporary office: frustration with computer programs, anger at crashing networks, and panic about the rapid rate of technological change (Fig. 3.10). Although all of those tensions arise out of multiple and complex causes, the collapse of the interface constitutes a key force in articulations of contemporary office work. We have to recognize that more effective documenta-

Fig. 3.10. Shrinking desk battle in *Brazil* (Milchan & Gilliam, 1985).

tion or even more effective, usable interfaces will not resolve the complex social, cognitive, emotional, and economic problems situated in both micro- and macrocontexts and the breakdowns among various aspects of the two. Effective work, Selber (2004) noted, requires that attention be paid not merely to functional literacies, but also to rhetorical and critical literacies. Inadequacies in any of these three aspects can have profound effects on the work, the worker, and the contexts in which they work.

The surfaced computer interface articulates computer work in two paradoxical directions (while simultaneously hiding the paradox): It purports to not merely support, but to show users how to complete a dizzying array of tasks while it decontextualizes and oversimplifies them. The interface articulates a tightly bounded space; because there is not room in that space to support rich complexity for all types of work, the complexity is stripped away, streamlining work. Users are often articulated here as workers without memory: Everything necessary is shown at the appropriate instant and removed when not necessary.

Such interfaces are not adequate to supporting the sorts of complex tasks increasingly required for many people. For example, Mirel (2003) posed the enormous complexity and contingency involved in what might be conceived of as a very simple task: selecting the mix of shortening and oils to stock in a grocery store chain. The task requires the user to make numerous comparisons of different datasets for products (ranging from sales figures, supplier data, profits, regional and national stocks); analyzing the accuracy of models offered by visualization software (which sometimes supply flawed visualizations), changing axes, weightings, and charts in visualizations; performing queries using visual manipulation (drilling down, storing data); and composing during data analysis (saving views, annotating data, storing data for review). Even the relatively advanced visualization software used in the scenario Mirel described (a far cry from standard spreadsheet or word processor interfaces) is incapable of supporting many of the tasks undertaken by the manager in this type of work.

Interface as Social Space

The previous sections illustrated a general trend in computer-supported learning that tends to isolate and fragment work from preexisting social contexts. Learning how to use a computer, for example, moved gradually from face-to-face apprenticeship models to computer-contained models in which the computer provided education. During the last decade, information about using the computer has undergone a subsequent shift, with networks socializing the interface. In socialized, networked interfaces, users have access to learning in an increasing number of spaces: not only depth (tutorial) and surfaced information (menus, toolbars, tooltips), but also access to other users.

As I mentioned briefly at the beginning, I see the possibility for recontextualizing work through interfaces. The Internet (WWW, MOO, IM, e-mail, etc.) is both a cause of the problem—because it collapses space—but also a possible remediation—because it may provide ways to resituate work into a social context by thinking of work as a process that goes on over time, as fundamentally communicative.

I am going to draw on graphical MOO interfaces to illustrate how the learning and work adapt to flattened spaces. MOOs are virtual environments in which users move around and interact with objects in a metaphoric space—users can type commands like "go north"; as you move north, you see textual or visual descriptions of a new place just north of where you previously were. The earliest MOOs and MUDS were developed and used by Dungeons and Dragons (D&D) types to enter into fantasy worlds and do virtual battles with monsters and, later, each other. The 1980s-era text adventure software Zork was a commercial progenitor to D&D (Zork grew out of Adventure, a Unix game developed by BBN programmer William Crowther as a hobby to distract himself from a failed marriage; Adams, n.d./2004). Contemporary MOOs articulate themselves as both a flattened surface (in their GUI formats) and a deep, apprenticeship space.

Currently, however, MOOs are much more complex and generalized and have been used extensively in computers and writing as well as law, second language learning, and more. The version of the MOO software used in these examples is Holmevick and Haynes' (2004) enCore Xpress, an open source MOO client that provides a graphical interface rather than a command-line interface (Fig. 3.11). The interface surfaces key commands, provides a running log of discussion, and provides graphical icons denoting objects within the environment (ranging from co-users to virtual tape recorders, desks, and other things) (Fig. 3.12).

In this example, the MOO is being used in a technical writing course, where students working in semiprivate team rooms are working on a report for a client who wants their Web site upgraded. Students are meeting in a virtual classroom and discussing their plans for a recommendation report written to a real-world client who wants a revised Web site. During their discussion, they are both talking (or typing) back and forth, but also entering text onto a virtual blackboard that will act as the starting point to their actual report.

Fig. 3.11. Graphical interface in ProNoun, running enCore Xpress (Holmevick & Haynes, 2004) showing command icons, object/user icons, and text discussion area.

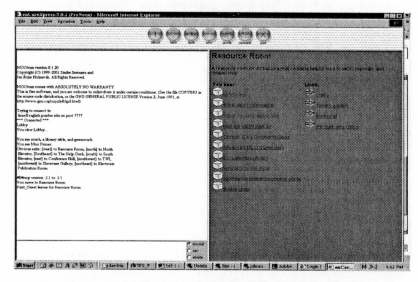

Fig. 3.12. Students working on technical writing project in MOO (object/user icons hidden) running enCore Xpress client (Holmevick & Haynes, 2004).

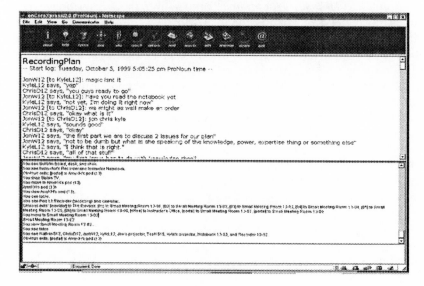

```
JonW12 [to KyleL12]: magic, isnt it
KyleL12 says, "yep"
ChrisD12 says, "you guys ready to go"
JonW12 [to KyleL12]: have you read the notebook yet
KyleL12 says, "not yet, I'm doing it right now"
JonW12 [to ChrisD12]: we might as well make an order
ChrisD12 says, "okay, what is it"
JohnW12 [to ChrisD12]: jon chris kyle
KyleL12 says, "sounds good"
ChrisD12 says, "okay"
JonW12 asys, "the first part we are to discuss 2 issues
for our plan"
JonW12 says, "not to be dumb but what is she speaking
of the knowledge, power, expertise thing or something
else"
KyleL12 says, "I think that is right"
ChrisD12 says, "all of that stuff"
```

Students, obviously, are not doing anything radically new here—these general types of projects have been used for many decades by technical communication teachers. Yet in terms of the microcontext, there are several important developments in interfaces such as this. First, as with Dreamweaver and other contemporary interfaces, what was once a depth-based model of learning and a sequential model of interaction is now a surfaced space. Early MOO programs—and many still in use today—work under the Telnet protocol and frequently involve command-line activities. These early spaces frequently focused on fantasy gaming. Although many still deal with warriors and ogres, the concept of MOO has been rearticulated in many contexts to involve educational uses rather than gaming. In a GUI-based MOO, such as enCore eXpress, learning about the interface is surfaced in the form of always-present, onscreen buttons for standard commands, menu headings, and visible representations of people and objects within the MOO as icons. At the same time, the surfaced interface is wrapped around (complexly, recursively) a deeper space; in a somewhat ambivalent way, the MOO embraces the push toward surfacing information while it attempts to develop a deeper, navigable space of social information. The microcontext begins to turn itself inside out. Notably, however, although basic work such as interaction in these spaces can be navigated primarily by typical user experience (i.e., someone with basic computer experience) coupled with on-screen suggestions, advanced work such as creating new spaces in the MOO typically requires traditional programming skills. This is not to condemn text-based MOOs for elitism—the social structure of most MOOs encourages new users to learn advanced skills with help from the broader community. Yet MOOs generally cannot support advanced work within the surfaced interface that greets novice users.

The interface to an enCore XPress interface can be locally rearticulated by users to some extent. For example, the prior screen has hidden the object/user icon pane that can be used to provide more screen real estate for other elements. Users can dismiss the Web browser interface entirely and work with a standard, character-based Telnet feed. In such an articulation, the interface is transformed into a version of the buried information interface described previously. In addition, MOO spaces contribute to the rearticulations of other technologies such as IM, which allow users to move from room to room (an activity that used to be called *switching channels* in earlier versions of IRC [Internet Relay Chat], the software that led to IM).

Such interfaces are the latest in a developing attempt for the computer to not merely be a support for learning and work, an artifact or tool, but to become a robust space for learning and work. The increasing use of such spaces (and parallel but different developments in instant messaging, avatars, etc.) belongs to an economic shift away from the production of industrial objects—cars, clothes, ping pong balls—and toward the production of symbolic information. Such people work within information ecologies (Nardi & O'Day, 2000) that themselves come to resemble—occurring within, across, and alongside the more familiar, concrete ecologies of our communities and parks.

The articulation of interface as flattened surface and deep social space comes at a price. The amount of screen real estate required to support GUI MOO interfaces with the space needed for various types of interactivity cannot also include more advanced work.

More to the point, symbolic-analytic work relies on the ability to move across and within information spaces with great speed. Although MOOs provide some facilities for symbolic-analytic work work, they cannot keep up with advanced demands. The MOO is articulated primarily as a social space, which is both its strength and weakness.

In a recursive way, the virtual context of the MOO is increasingly fragmented in the form of IM sessions, which reclaim the real-time chat facilities that earlier spawned MOOspaces.[8] IM sessions break down the virtual contexts of MOOspace and colonize larger working and learning spaces: Students in classes and workers in offices engage in IM sessions that occur in the gaps in their real work, switching among numerous contexts (the official space of writing a report in Word). Articulations of symbolic-analytic space are never stable nor are they on a linear trajectory leading to some perfect, seamless communication. Articulations, like deconstructions, are always ongoing disarticulations and rearticulations.

Notes

1.   Consider the effect of Gibson's (1984) highly influential cyberpunk novel *Neuromancer* on an entire generation of programmers and interface design-ers who took up Gibson's narrative text and attempted to make it operational. Ironically, Gibson knew little about computers and wrote his first novel on a typewriter. Some have suggested his remove from the computing communi-ty gave him freedom to envision a new way of working (although there were numerous other VR narrative and film descriptions prior to Gibson's work—the movie *Tron*, Vernor Vinge's science fiction novel *True Names*, etc.).

2.   Bolter and Grusin's (2000) *Remediations* is one of the best attempts to exam-ine the implications of these two perspectives.

3.   This articulation of *interface* is still common in many hardware-related fields such as computer engineering. The term *communication* likewise is articulat-ed in different ways in computer engineering and technical communication. Historically, the term has occupied a nexus point among disciplines in artic-ulations such as Shannon and Weaver's (1949) mathematical theory of com-munication, developed in terms of electronic signal processing in telephony and being imported into communication theory.

4.   Evolution in the sense of gradual change, but not in the modernist sense of working toward some teleological perfection.

5.   At Clarkson University, systems administrator Brian Huntley's e-mail .sig reads, "UNIX *is* user friendly. It's just selective about who its friends are."

6.   This expertise level might have been accurate at the time I created the rollover images several years ago. The features I identify here that helped me integrate the rollovers have also made their use relatively common on the Web.

7.   The point here is not that specific workers do not have a responsibility to work within certain boundaries, but that the manager would translate time away from the desk automatically into poor performance rather than a pos-sible attempt to learn something work-related.

8.   In an important sense, IM-type interactivity predates the origins of the MOO, with a MOO being something like an extension of the older UNIX "talk" com-mand and Internet Relay Chat (IRC). So in one way of thinking, UNIX talk and IRC branched into the development of an eventually surfaced form in graph-ical MOOs and the development of a fragmented form in Instant Messenger.

4

INTERFACE OVERFLOW

Tools always presuppose a machine, and the machine is always social
before being technical. There is always a social machine which selects
or assigns the technical elements used. A tool remains marginal, or little used, until there exists a social machine or collective assemblage
which is capable of taking it into its "phylum."
—Deleuze and Parnet (1989, p. 70)

Although the interfaces discussed in the previous chapter struggle to contain the amount of information users need, we can learn a great deal by
stepping back and considering the interface in its local, physical contexts.
The interface and the work done in it are articulated in and by those contexts. The analysis of these microcontexts extends observations in the last
chapter about the collapse of learning and work into the interface, but it
also suggests some countertrends. In this chapter, I look at how different
forms of work (and workers) are articulated with different interfaces.

"WORK WITH STUFF":
A SPACE FOR ACADEMIC THEORY AND RESEARCH

Talking one day with Brent Faber, a colleague in the Technical
Communications Department at Clarkson University, I noticed a whiteboard hanging on his office wall displaying a chart showing where various
projects were in the drafting and publication process. I set up an formal
interview with Brent so I could better document the information space that
he had developed for working.

During the interview, Brent described six connected functional information spaces, each possessing different but overlapping functionalities.

For example, in addition to commonly understood information spaces such as bookshelves and computers, Brent works extensively with an information work table (consisting of stacks of notecards and books), a large whiteboard, and a chalkboard (see Fig. 4.1).

Brent explained that he uses the whiteboard to hold what he thinks are emergent, partially formed, but potentially important ideas. He keeps

Fig. 4.1. Map of Faber's office.

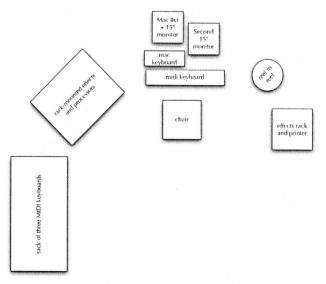

these ideas on the whiteboard for days or weeks, where he uses the omnipresent display to cue thinking and rethinking over time. Eventually, he transfers the ideas from the whiteboard to two separate, simultaneously active workspaces: a chalkboard that holds a rough timeline of his ongoing research and publication projects as well as a computer file, usually in WordPerfect, that he uses to begin drafting a research article, book chapter, grant proposal, or other communication. Notably, many of the artifacts and fragmentary texts in his office—notecards, writing on chalkboard and whiteboard, texts—are functionally indexical, pointing to other objects to facilitate tracking, filtering, and rearrangement.

These processes are neither neat nor linear—a fact that is true of writing in general. Of paramount importance for Faber—and symbolic-analytic workers in general—is the ability to have information spread around the workspace, migrating from space to space, pooling temporarily during the course of differing aspects of the project (see Figs. 4.2 and 4.3).

What I've thought to do . . . is to have data here [points to table] and then workspace, writing space here [points to computer desk], and I can freely move back and forth. [says data is] print, stuff, texts, books, notes, archival stuff, all the stuff that I'm going to use to write. I always have a problem because I write from . . . from stuff. My good writing is always from stuff, I'm an empiricist.

Fig. 4.2. Faber discussing information work objects in office space.

When you're doing theory . . . I find, anyway, doing theory, the greatest criticism is that you don't have any data. So I think it's always important to buffer the data . . . . So I try to make sure I have stuff.

Fig. 4.3. Faber describing use of "big ideas" space.

Faber's work—research-based writing—requires support for extremely complex, contingent, and data-driven activities spread over a wide space (both virtual and concrete). Such relatively complex, interconnected methods of working are increasingly common.

INFORMATION OVERFLOW: PROTOOLS AND MUSIC COMPOSITION

In the winter and spring of 2001, I began working with David Dies, a graduate student at the Crane School of Music at SUNY Potsdam. David works extensively in ProTools; during the sessions I observed, David was composing a commissioned work for CD and trumpet. The project consisted of two main parts: an electronically authored, recorded CD as well as a score for live trumpet. David composes the CD tracks in ProTools, relying on several MIDI keyboards connected to the workstation running ProTools. David spends an enormous amount of time manipulating—cutting and pasting, applying filters, multi-tracking, and rearranging various aspects of the online information—to arrive at a final (or one possible final) piece of music that is then burned to CD (see Fig 4.4).

Fig.4.4. Dense, surface information in Protocols (Digidesign, 2001).

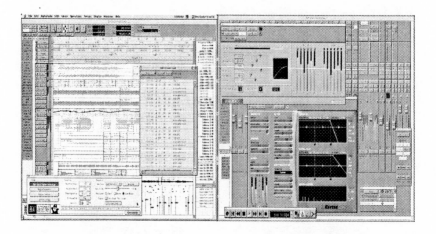

ProTools can seem rather disconcerting to users used to relatively information-sparse or even hierarchically organized interfaces such as Microsoft Word, which might contain a great deal of information, but arrange that information in ways that make it easy to focus on the main work area (e.g., the text being typed onto a page). ProTools seems remarkably packed with information. In the screenshot shown here (taken from ProTools' Web site, < http://www.digidesign.com/ >), images from two physical computer monitors have been arranged side by side, information from the main screen spilling over into another physical screen to provide a doubled digital information space.

The increase in size of interface has been a relatively constant trend in computer technologies. The earliest laptop I owned, a Tandy 100, sported a tiny eight-line by 40 character LCD display. My desktop configuration today (15 years later) includes a 15-inch LCD laptop display augmented by a 21-inch monitor to provide a virtually continuous display of approximately 2 1/2 foot by 1 foot (2,560 pixels by 1,878 pixels). Projection systems for desktop use are increasingly popular. The computer lab I use on our campus offers a 72-inch rear-projection, touchscreen computer run from an infrared keyboard.[1]

In an interface such as ProTools (and opposed to programs like Word, Internet Explorer, or even Instant Messenger [IM]), the focus of work is not the production of original text (a term that is somewhat suspect, even if not questioned). In ProTools, although there are some facilities for the generation of original information (through, for example, line inputs for microphones and instruments), the program and interface focus primarily on the manipulation of information: cut and paste, rearrangement, filtering, compressing, and recombining tones and rhythms, postmodern forms of work. Dies' use of ProTools as an environment for symbolic-analytic work rather than simple record is relatively common.

In an interview with the band Oysterhead about their use of ProTools, drummer Stewart Copeland describes the process of working with a nonlinear digital audio system such as ProTools:

> A lot of the material was arrived at by us jamming indeterminably and then cutting to the chase. Of course, that involves editing. . . . Once we cut together the cool stuff, we'd figure out a lyric, and then sometimes we'd go play it again having worked it out. And sometimes what we played initially was the track. The only thing then was assembling the backing tracks; and then, at that point, it was overdubs just like any album process.

We started with about three days of jamming, and then a day cutting, and then another three days jamming and then another day cutting. . . . A lot of times, I'd be cutting in the morning. They'd roll in in the afternoon and I'd cut files in the morning.[2]

ProTools, as described by most users including David, provides a different order of space for composing and editing music—one that allows the construction of a pool of musical fragments, generated either by breaking down preexisting long threads (as described in the quote earlier from Stewart Copeland) or playing discontinuous, divided notes existing initially only as fragments to be modified, transformed, filtered, stretched, and recombined.

In some sessions, David worked primarily at the ProTools computer workstation, although in many instances he alternated between typing on the computer keyboard and playing notes on the MIDI keyboard that served as a workdesk for the computer, among other things.

During a single, 2-minute section of one session, Dies moves from focusing across both computer screens, his watch, a handwritten notebook, and both a computer keyboard and a MIDI keyboard. The boundaries of the interface have functionally disintegrated: Information is not contained merely within the interface (or even spread among many interfaces among Internetworked connections). Information spills over the edges of this interface, with Dies working within an information environment that grows out of, includes, and is affected by information and actions both within and without the interface.

Although work in ProTools is interesting to me simply because of the sheer amount of surfaced information present, I was also struck by the ways that information about David's work was spread not merely across two screens, but around his immediate work environment (see Figs. 4.5 and 4.6). At times he strides around the room with a notebook, making and referring to notes about filters, keyboards, and structures (see Fig. 4.7). Although the resulting musical composition will be a linear piece, the structure of the composing process is remarkably nonlinear and recursive, relying on a complex series of repetitions, filters, manipulations, and structurings.

During our first session, David began by opening a new file in ProTools and then creating eight blank tracks. He is creating, he says, "a canvas and a palette" that will eventually hold interesting chunks of sound that he thinks he might use.[3] During these initial sessions, he has a rough idea of the piece, but concentrates on experimenting with different tambres.[4] Characteristic of new forms of work, David's composition process relies frequently—although not primarily—on chance and relative chaos as he experiments with different sounds.

Fig. 4.5. David Dies working at ProTools workstation.

Fig. 4.6. Layout of David Dies' workspace.

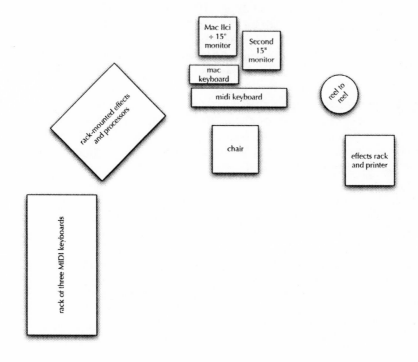

Fig. 4.7. David Dies moving around workspace.

      After setting up the blank palette in ProTools, he left the worksta-
tion and moved to a rack of three MIDI keyboards, where he spent most of
the hour during my initial session with him.

      For nearly all of the first hour of the session, David repeated a simple
process over and over: He played a single note on one of the MIDI keyboards, paused, played the next higher note on the scale, paused, played
the next higher note, usually stringing together four to six notes on a scale.
The complexity of the sounds built as he began applying patches with different filters and envelopes, the pattern of the attack and decay envelopes
shifting as he manipulated the controls on the keyboard. When he initially
picked up the notepad, he explained,

> I don't do a lot of sketchpad work, but I usually will get a list of colors.
> If I don't . . . I don't know what I 'm going to do with that sound, but
> I like that sound. . . . So I'm going to write down the name of the thing,
> and its patch.

> A lot of this work just ends up being cutting and pasting. So I've creat-
> ed that shape; I like the reverse in the other one. It gives it just a sub-
> tle variety against the original. I transposed it up a half step to give it a
> little . . . um. aural shift. And now I'm pasting that in. I'm going to cre-
> ate a rhythm by pasting another one so . . . at the outset, beginning of
> the second chunk.

The sounds were not notes or chords in the traditional understanding of music composition, but material meant to be broken apart, recombined, and additionally manipulated:

> Usually when I'm building a palette like this what I'll do is . . . of something this boring . . . is just record a long chunk so that I have something that I can extract from easily later. And I'll do the same interval at different levels on the keyboard so that I . . . A lot of tambres will create a different color.
>
> [plays a tone]
>
> This is much warmer.

What is interesting about the process is the way that David creates structure with methods that are recursive, contingent, experimental, and nonlinear. Perhaps more important, the process relies heavily on David's ability to generate, manipulate, transform, and arrange information in an information space that is both densely packed and spatially distributed. Although there are obvious structures and organization at work here—It is not pure anarchic chaos—such forms of working and thinking forefront their contingency in primary ways.

One is reminded of Jackson Pollock's massive abstract expressionist works, densely packed with random spatters of multicolored paint. In one sense, David's process does resemble Pollock's. In another important sense, however, Pollock's work attempted to capture Truth by removing premeditation or mediation; David's work is anything but unmediated. Chance juxtapositions of notes are captured, analyzed, cut apart, and recombined in new ways. Contingency is not a provisional window toward some higher meaning, but a simple fact, an aspect of work. In a later session, David looks to the camera and explains,

> I've pasted some I'm transposing that transition so you get a creeping, but a pulsing, larger shape? [gesticulating wildly with hands]
>
> I kind of like that as a fundamental sound . . . but I'm going to be adding some layers for interest . . . um . . . that thumpier sound you heard earlier with a higher . . . sort of a . . . percussion . . . sound over the top of that as sort of a sweep and probably lay in a subtone . . . a low . . . kind of humming sound. Which I need to find yet.

Information is not a tool, record, or plan of work: It is the environment for work and the work itself: the datacloud. Moreover, information is not something to be rigorously controlled and structured; it is not something to be easily understood; it is something to be played with, challenged and confused by, experimented with, and transformed. These are all aspects of postmodern work.

SPACES FOR SYMBOLIC-ANALYTIC WORK: VIRTUAL AND REAL

As Spinuzzi (2003) noted in his study of programmers, *Tracing Genres Through Organizations,* workers in information-rich environments deal with an enormous range of communication artifacts throughout their day. Adequately supporting that work—not merely at the functional level, but at all levels—requires that we learn ways of understanding how that work takes place. The computer interface was once a calculation device—an artifact enmeshed in a social context. During the last five decades of the 20th century, the computer began to absorb and contain not merely the objects being worked on (equations, word-processed documents, Web pages), but also meta-information about those objects, including structures and procedures for learning and working. In other words, the computer and space around it began to absorb and then reflect back context. In many instances, the reflections have taken on significations divorced of any original context—the "crop" tool, for example, in PageMaker emulates a physical device used by graphic artists—a set of sliding, joined, right-angle rods that can be open or closed to allow rectangular cuts to be made on subportions of an image to remove irrelevant material at the edges of frames (see Fig. 4.8). What percentage of current users of this program are aware of an earlier tool?[5] Not only do users of the current program usually lack the social context in which the earlier technology was used—they lack the community of education that provided support to novices learning printing and graphic arts, to teach them complex design issues, professional ethics, and other skills not present within the limited space of the interface.

In the end, the computer is not capable of supporting the amount of information necessary for contemporary work, either at the macro- or microlevel. As a networked device, the interface offers a portal for users to connect up to other users in a virtual collaborative space for learning and work. As a locally contextualized object, the interface becomes enmeshed with a functional information context—one that denies exclusively on- or offline information.

Fig. 4.8. Crop tool (selected) in Adobe PageMaker toolbar.

The space here departs from current notions about virtual reality. If this is a city, it is one designed less from the relatively comfortable, just-like-the-real-world (but-shinier) virtual architecture of Mitchell's (1996) *City of Bits* and more like the postmodern architecture of Tschumi's (1996) glass video gallery—both depth and surface. Mitchell's popular meditation on the architectures of virtual communities attempts to reconstruct virtual space along traditionally architectural lines, with virtual spaces offering dramatic but nonrevolutionary improvements over our existing spaces:

> As the development of pioneering campus and community networks has already suggested, there will be an important role here for local subnetworks of the national and international systems—electronic Main Streets that provide places for citizens to present themselves in their communities, to exchange greetings and gossip with neighbors, and to transact local business. Bitsphere civic design will encompass not only traditional matters of roads and sidewalks, sewers, and land-use zoning, but also the development of local network infrastructure and creation of electronic venues for local communication and interaction. (Mitchell, 1996, p. 170)

People here tend more toward industrial, routine production or in-person service work than symbolic-analytic, perpetuating a happy (and unreal) world of a high-tech Norman Rockwell.

The information ecologies analyzed by Nardi and O'Day (2000) are articulated in a similar fashion. Although they highlighted some significant potential social issues in their discussions of networked collaborative spaces, they also use real worlds as their models:

> The Internet is a vast playing field for diversity. It is a library, a marketplace, a post office, a retail shop, a broadcast service, and much more. Huge as it is, the Internet paradoxically underwrites diversity and the emergence of local information ecologies by providing a publishing forum for anyone with a computer and a modem. The Internet is a giant network, but each node can be as small as one person or interest group. The Internet bypasses the bottleneck of the mass media (and government censorship in some cases) that so constrains expression. It is a medium in which we are seeing a return to handcrafted information—as though letter writing, pamphleteering, and afternoon watercolor painting are given new life. The letters are e-mail messages, the pamphlets are posts to newsgroups, and the watercolors are digital photos now, but they are animated by the same spirit of personal expression. (p. 214)

There is something both comfortably optimistic and vaguely unsettling about these visions of technological cultures. On the one hand, it seems absolutely crucial that we work to envision contexts in which technologies are integrated into humane, empowering, and ethical activities and relationships. On the other hand, it also seems absolutely crucial that we recognize the disruptive potential of technologies, the point of, to use Joyce's (1996) phrase, "the momentary advantage of our awkwardness" in which one set of articulations might be made in different ways. These emergent symbolic-analytic spaces have more in common with deconstructive architecture than modernist—more like Bernard Tschumi's disconcertingly powerful glass video gallery (see Fig. 4.9). Inhabitants in such spaces are challenged by what we used to think of as information overload, a situation that symbolic-analytic workers have learned to use to their advantage. As Jameson (1991) argued of postmodernist cultures, symbolic-analytic spaces require inhabitants to gain the ability to cognitively map themselves in relation to vast and contingent information spaces—a simultaneously necessary and impossible task, more of an ongoing process than a goal.

I return to Tschumi's work in a later chapter to consider the possibilities of deconstructive architecture as an approach to interface design. Briefly put, work such as Tschumi's provides an interesting response to the

Fig.4.9. Tschumi's (1996) Glass Video Gallery.

current functionalist approach to computer interface design because it rejects the notion that architecture should or even can be solely functional. Tschumi's work attempts to challenge preconceptions; it also challenges occupants to re-understand their own activities. They exhibit, in philosophical terms, a surplus of meaning. They offer spaces of information overload—environments with contingent, shifting meanings rather than neatly ordered rows.

The information spaces I have been described in this chapter and toward the end of the previous one constitute paradigmatic spaces for symbolic-analytic work. In Dies' and Faber's offices, we find traditional computing technologies, but we also find an environment saturated with information, both within the computer and without. These spaces prioritize fluid movement of information and, just as important, the ability of users to move around within that information space. Rather than trying to order information, users within these spaces explicitly disorder information, and push it around in streams, letting it stand temporarily in pools to see what develops. Faber's idea board, for example, supported hazy, tentative "big ideas" that may or may not pan out. By sketching them on a chalkboard, they remained visible continuously; they were part of the information space, but in a contingent pool so that, over time, Faber could mentally bring together the information on the board with information from other spaces (the work table, the computer, the bookshelves, the phone). Dies space, like Faber's, included numerous writing surfaces; it also included musical instruments, which he used for playing basic tones that he listened to, took notes on, and occasionally imported into the computer for manipulation. Dies' creation of these tones is particularly interesting because his work with the MIDI keyboards resembled something closer to pushing buttons than playing music.[6] Although some might criticize this form of composition, the most substantial composing involved manipulation of those tones on the computer and in his notes.

This sort of work has been characterized by Mirel (2003) as complex problem solving—an activity that she notes is not well supported by existing interfaces. Complex problems are defined by Mirel as having these characteristics:

> Ill-defined solutions and goals
> Tied to the interests of diverse stakeholders
> Complex information from many sources
> Dynamic and emergent
> No pre-set entry points or stopping points
> Iterative and opportunistic with socially based patterns of inquiry
> "Good enough" solutions with no one right answer. (p. 22)

Unfortunately, current approaches to computers in education tend to prioritize more traditional types of work: writing essays and reports in word processors, analyzing profit and loss flows in spreadsheets, and calculating forces in numerical analysis programs. These are all useful skills, but they are the legacy of an earlier form of work—one that is being replaced by more complex forms. Because we have failed to understand the characteristics of symbolic-analytic work, we have yet to do an effective job of helping people learn to become symbolic-analytic workers.[7] Take computer-supported classrooms, for example.

Our current models of computer-supported learning spaces tend toward providing access to technologies, the more advanced the better. The lab in which I teach possesses a room full of (in today's terms or at least last year's) relatively speedy, well-equipped computers hosting a healthy roster of professional-level communication and design software. In fact the computers within this lab are several generations beyond the computer David Dies used to run ProTools (which involved the connection of tens of thousands of dollars of digital musical equipment to a 1990-era Macintosh IIci). From the perspective of symbolic-analytic work, at least, Dies' work is more advanced despite its less powerful computing equipment.

COMPRESSING SYMBOLIC-ANALYTIC WORKSPACE

Because we fail to understand how people work with and within information space, we also often fail to adequately support that work. At the same time, it is easy to miss the fact that symbolic-analytic work requires a much larger and more complex information space than can be supported by the computer alone. The front half of the teaching lab is arranged, as many such labs are, in short rows that appear to insist users focus on the screen in front of them. The screen is considered the primary location for working and learning, as illustrated during an interview with Ryan McDougall, a student communication specialist who works in the lab.

As I was returning from interviewing Faber, I took a shortcut through the computer lab and was startled, halfway through the darkened lab, to find Ryan seated in front of a computer, working in Photoshop with all the lights in the lab turned off. When I asked him why the lights were out, he said that,

> One, I don't know, it helps me see the screen a little better. But, two, it keeps people from bothering me, trying to get into the [lab].

Although the lab is in high demand, the staffing budget does not allow the lab to be open continually (and the amount of high-end equipment within it prevents opening without staff to both monitor security and help users work with the technologies). This situation presents a dilemma: Student employees are offered the perk of after-hours access to the lab so they can work on their own projects. Yet if other potential users are in the lab, the student employees—who are off the clock at that point—end up providing technical and communication support to students, which interrupts their own work. (The student employees, including Ryan, frequently donate their time to keep the lab open after official hours, although they occasionally also choose to keep the doors locked if they are working toward a deadline and will not have time to offer assistance to other users.) Ryan's solution—leaving the lights off so people on the outside would be less likely to notice that the lab was occupied and, in theory, open—highlights how our conceptions of work have been constructed. Ryan made a clear distinction between the work he was completing for the Center and the work he often completes as a student. For the latter, which I observed, he occupies a small, isolated space: The cubicle-shaped desk provides him with approximately 6 square feet of desk space, including room taken up by the computer keyboard and a bulky, 19-inch CRT monitor. All work was focused within the computer interface. Although Ryan had with him a notebook related to his work, it seemed clear that he was not going to be doing much work that was not displayed on the glowing computer monitor (see Fig. 4.10).

Fig. 4.10. Ryan McDougall discussing configuration of workspace in campus computer lab.

If he needs to work with a notebook or other texts, Ryan explained, he moves the keyboard aside, takes a specific text from his bookbag, consults the text to look up information or record notes, replaces the notebook into the bookbag, and pulls the keyboard back out to continue work. Because the lights were off, even that minimal workspace was relatively useless for information work because the glow of the CRT did not provide enough light to read or write in a notebook. The routine nature of such work is supported adequately (if a little compactly) by the space he occupies. Two tendential forces participate in constructing Ryan's work here: the architecture of the information space he works and the particular task he had been assigned to do.

The scene in which Ryan worked recalls many scenes in the dystopian film, *Brazil* (Milchan & Gilliam, 1985), in which Terry Gilliam satirizes office workspaces through such advanced technologies as magnifying lenses that fit over too-small computer monitors and battles over desktop space between two adjoining office workers who must share a single desk, divided by the wall that separates them.

More important, the main protagonist in *Brazil*, like Ryan McDougal, does only simple tasks within this workspace. Quite apart from the need for character and plot development, offices in *Brazil* do not support complex work involving the movement of information from different sources (Table 4.1).

Table 4.1 Microcontexts and Interfaces for Observed Work

	Category of Work	Physical Workspace	Primary Interface
Faber	Symbolic-analytic	Large and complex	Linear (WordPerfect)
Dies	Symbolic-analytic	Large and complex	Complex (ProTools + MIDI keyboards)
McDougal	Routine production	Small and simplified	Medium complex (Photoshop)

RETURNING TO THE LAB:
REARTICULATING STUDENT WORK SPACES

The first sketch in Fig 4.11 shows a portion of the space in which Ryan worked, a 22-seat teaching lab composed of rows of computers separated by low dividers. The workspaces measure 4 feet wide by 2 feet deep. To the left and right of each individual workspace stands a low, curved dividing wall. At the back of each work area that does not sit against a wall is a slightly taller divider (approximately a foot and a half high) that, not coincidentally, minimizes the frequency with which one user catches the eye of the user directly across from him or her. CPUs for systems reside in tower cases on the floor; the horizontal counters on which the 19-inch CRT monitors sit also hold an extended keyboard, mouse, and mouse pad as well as either an 8" x 10" Wacom graphics tablet or an HP ScanJet scanner. On average, these workstations provide less than 2 square feet of open surface area that can hold papers, books, or other user items (see Fig. 4.12).

The architecture of this particular workspace is strikingly different from that of people like David Dies, Brent Faber, or other symbolic-analytic workers. Ryan's working space is very small, with the focal point on the

Fig. 4.11. Portion of map of CEC teaching lab with Ryan worked.

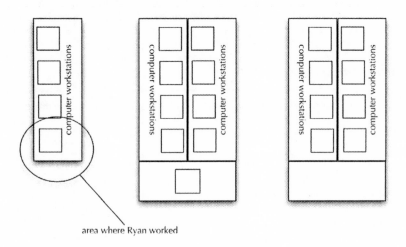

area where Ryan worked

Fig. 4.12. Map of Ryan's workspace (detail).

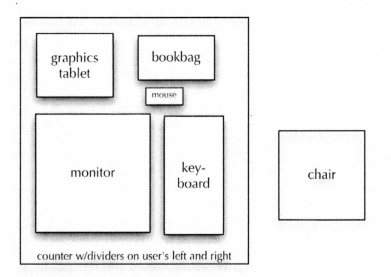

computer. At most Ryan can overlap windows on the screen to gain spaces for different information flows and pools (which may explain why IM use is so popular in such spaces—it provides a simple communication stream that is small and fragmented enough it can coexist with the other workspaces on the small CRT). Even if the lights were on and Ryan could see enough to use the notebook he had with him, there was painfully little space for him to spread notebooks out to construct other information spaces that seem necessary to creative problem solving of the sort that symbolic analysts do.

Second, the tasks that we had asked Ryan to do were of the sort that *could* be supported by such limited information spaces: the editing of graphics for a Web site. Although this task requires a relatively high degree of technical expertise, it is also routine. In a sense, we have articulated symbolic-analytic work into a routine-production activity space.

It was not until several weeks after the interview—during my analysis of the video and the construction of transcripts—that I realized Ryan had settled on this space because the task was so rudimentary it did not require a complex, large information space. The lab is actually constructed to support multiple types of work—the front half of the lab, where Ryan worked, supports technology training as well as a request for spaces in which students would require privacy (hence the dividers between workstations). This particular part of the lab was designed not for complex work, but for students to learn simple technical skills or take online tests. This purpose allowed the building planners to increase the density of workstations per foot in one part of the lab so they could allow more square footage per computer in other areas of the lab (see Fig. 4.13).

As the map of the lab shows, we have attempted to construct different architectures to support different kinds of work. The front half of the lab (the Bay Area), where Ryan was working while I interviewed him, exemplifies traditional thinking about computer-supported learning spaces: pack as much high technology as you can within the space. The back half of the lab, however, begins to support symbolic-analytic work in important ways. There are spaces for digital video production, focus group videotaping, usability testing, and teamwork and informal project meetings (see Fig. 4.14).

A usability lab provides multiple information and communication spaces for helping students and faculty understand how real users interact with Web sites and other online materials they have designed. Several remote-controlled cameras can pan and zoom to gather information streams of users in addition to a monitor feed split off from the user's computer to record on-screen actions, as well as both a 10-square-foot window and an intercom system.

Fig. 4.13. Map of different workspaces within the Eastman Kodak Center for Excellence in Communication.

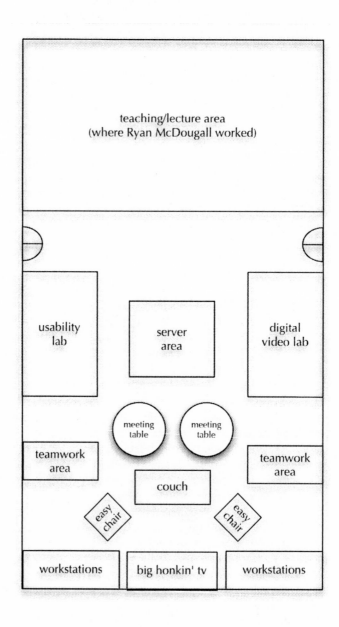

Fig. 4.14. Usability testing lab.

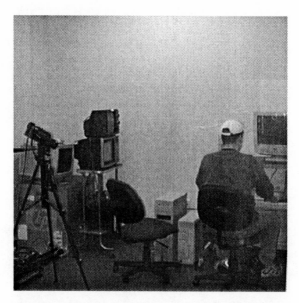

Toward the back of the CEC, the space has been structured to support team-based work and the multiple streams of information, ranging from horizontal surfaces for spreading out printouts, books, charts, and other crucial information sources (including Ethernet ports and a wireless hub so that laptop computers can be dropped into the campus network; see Fig. 4.15).

The back of the room provides one of the largest information spaces, what we fondly refer to as The Big Honkin' TV (see Fig. 4.16): The SmartBoard system provides a 72-inch, rear-projection, touchscreen, intelligent whiteboard surface for work. I should admit that when the system, which was ordered before I arrived on campus, was delivered, I shuddered. Before it was connected, it seemed to be little more than a $12,000 TV suitable for watching the Canadian National hockey team during the winter olympics (an activity it supported well), but little else. The funds that purchased it, I thought to myself, could have purchased several servers or intermediate-level video-editing workstations.

Eventually, however, I began to have my students call up their Web site design projects on the BHTV, and I was amazed at the change in the environment. The size of the screen converted what might appear to be just a large display into an information space: Users seated 10 feet from the dis-

Fig. 4.15. Spaces for team-based work in the CEC.

Fig. 4.16. Students in the CEC working at the Big Honkin' TV.

play look *at* the screen, and users standing at the screen are *within* an information space, nearly literally laid across an information space. That space
is large enough to encompass more than one user. The first time I brought
a group of students to the space, three of them leapt up at once to begin
using the special whiteboard markers to begin sketching revision com-
ments onto the screen. In the front of the lab, team-based projects always
result in one person typing while the other team members remain seated
behind, vocal (at best, more often silent) but not involved in the manipulation of information on the screen.

The shift in screen size offers an example of how a relatively isolated
change in one aspect of a technical situation can dramatically rearticulate
the whole activity. As the area of the screen expands (from something on
the order of just over 2 square feet to 16 square feet), the information
space dominates the visual field. Unlike virtual reality systems, however,
the BHTV does not replace one reality with another, but rearranges existing reality across it. This may seem like a minor point until we recall that,
although we sometimes seem driven to translate everything into the virtual space of the computer, there continue to be many useful qualities of
what is sometimes derisively termed *meatspace*: the real world.

In addition, the space of information manipulation expands dramatically, with information work becoming a bodied experience. I would not
want to overemphasize the importance of direct manipulation of information, because *direct* represents a wildly relative term in information spaces.
Yet the consistent trend toward an increase in display space points to the
need for working with large amounts of information. In this case, the interface also affords the ability to include more than one person inside the
information space. What was previously, physically at least, an individually controlled technology is now a multiperson space. The space of the
image then becomes immersive in a way not available to teams of users in
front of even a standard-size monitor. The difference is related to that dividing cinema from TV, two media that seem little different on the surface
(indeed movies originating in the theater often end up on the video
screen), but afford a different engagement in practice (a point around
which much cinema theory revolves).

This rearticulation cannot be applied in just any architecture. All articulations are, to some extent, local and contingent. For example, many lecture
halls on campus provide large projection screens (some much larger than the
BHTV), but for various reasons they do not promote the same type of active
collaboration as I witnessed in front of the BHTV. For example, courses held
in large spaces often demand large data displays, but the number of students
in such a course promotes one-too-many lectures rather than discussion.[8]

I have occasionally given lectures using projected images on screens up to 35 feet wide, but the information space is normally not inhabited in the same way during these lectures. The focus of work oscillates constantly between screen and audience, and I feel that I am in a movie theater standing in front while the audience attempts to see the film around me. This lack of engagement or inhabitation of the projected visual space points to an important distinction between film and TV commonly made by cinema theorists: Viewers of films tend to occupy the visual space of the image, taking on the subject position of the camera within that space. The size of the image, the attempt to block out extraneous stimuli, and other techniques, including a cultural understanding of how film experiences *should* operate, all work to engage a film viewer in ways that TV does not.

Although it would be possible to hold much smaller, interactive, and collaborative classes in these large spaces, to do so would violate our institution's (and most academic institutions') goal of maximizing space usage: Small groups of students are not scheduled for large rooms so that those spaces remain free for large groups. Although on rare occasion a small class may use a large lecture hall, the infrequency of this event makes it unlikely that the data display would support direct manipulation by small groups. Further, lecturers might also use direct manipulation facilities individually, but the structure of such a course encourages extensive prior planning and preparation of material. The types of work my students undertook with the BHTV was, in contrast, dynamic and contingent.

We are attempting to understand how users move within information spaces, how users can exist *within* information spaces rather than merely gaze at them, and how information spaces must be shared with others rather than being private, lived within rather than simply visited. More important, we are also interested in moving beyond a notion of virtual or hybrid space that merely replicates our existing ways of living, communicating, and working.

VIRTUAL REALITY AND UBIQUITOUS COMPUTING: SOME SUGGESTIONS ABOUT MEDIATED, HETEROGENEOUS SPACES

[W]hat educators hold against VR is roughly equivalent to what the state holds against illicit drugs: they both challenge the reality principle.
—D. Davis (1998, p. 268)

More and more people are succumbing to so called "technology addictions," spending hours tapping on mobile phones or surfing the Internet, one of Britain's best known psychiatric clinics said on Saturday.

"There has been a huge rise in behavioral addictions," including excessive texting, said a spokeswoman for the Priory Clinic which treats 6,000 patients a year for a range of addictions including gambling, eating disorders and drugs.

In the Sunday Telegraph newspaper the head of the clinic's addictions unit said some patients were spending up to seven hours a day text messaging.

"We have a situation where some people look down on alcoholics and cocaine addicts, but then go and spend five hours in an Internet chat room," Dr Mark Collins told the paper.

—"Thumbs Down for Text Messages—They are Officially Addictive" (2003)

Text messages have superseded phone calls as the most common use for a mobile phone among young people, a new survey reveals.

—"Young 'Prefer Texting to Calls'," (2003)

The structure for a particular technology does not unilaterally determine how it is used any more than any individual user could pick up a random piece of technology and make it function in any way he or she wanted. Objects contain tendential forces that afford certain types of uses and discourage others; the same can be said for users and communities. Articulations are, in this way, both material and symbolic, and there is slippage in both, but rarely absolute free play (and frequently slippage can be minimal).

In the brief history sketched earlier, developments such as fragmented, decontextualized communication in programs like IM software are associated with parallel shifts in the structures of work and learning. Such forms of working and learning as a symptom of postmodern capitalism are described by groups as diverse as leftist literary critics, management theorists, economists, and others. Users in the spaces we have analyzed—both micro- and macrocontexts—work and learn within visually and structurally dense, often frankly and intentionally chaotic spaces. They multitask, surf, filter, push, and pull data streams. To such users, the distinctions between surface and depth make little sense. In fact the often-held separation between online and IRL is tenuous, with relationships developed online spilling over into the real world, and with information at the surface or at depth in the computer moving back and forth to PDA, Web-enabled phone, video monitor, stereo, and more.

In *Remediation,* Bolter and Grusin (2000) offered two opposing ways to understand new media: virtual reality and ubiquitous computing. In the former, designers attempt to create an online space so real that users work as if they were in a real space—as if the computer were not mediating reality. In the latter, designers explicitly forefront the mediated nature of the interface, layering and overlapping information in complex ways. A MOO interface tends toward a proto-VR category, whereas, the IM interface tends toward the ubiquitous computing realm. Drawing a hard and fast division between the two, however, has become increasingly difficult.

Instant messaging is frequently articulated as a way to rupture these limited spaces, occupying tiny gaps at the surface to link user to user. Whereas a MOOspace—especially a visual interface—requires a relatively large amount of screen real estate as well as relatively sustained attention over time, IM sessions are, by nature, sporadic and small grained. In effect, IM rearticulates communication in forms more amenable to both the pace of individual work contexts and the space of individual work environments.

Like all technology use (and all articulations), the specific processes and structures critically depend on local, concrete contexts. Although I suggested that IM use can be a rupturing event, a fragmentation, in many contexts IM is being articulated in ways that reign in resistant and subversive activities. Over the last several years, companies including Microsoft, Yahoo, IBM, and Jabber have been working to encourage corporate acceptance of the technology. This encouragement comes not merely from advertising products, but through a broad rearticulation, including both symbolic and material reworkings. In an article in the *eWeek,* Louderback (2003) offered several corporate benefits of IM:

> [T]here are some pretty sound reasons for [using IM]. The immediacy of instant messaging ensures that users will get the message as quickly as possible—and that it won't languish in an e-mail box for hours or days. Imagine an airline that needs to inform a range of people about a deal. A broadcast IM would be a good and immediate way to do it. Or maybe you subscribe to a news service where knowing something quickly can mean the difference between profit and loss.
>
> There are even more subtle uses. Perhaps there's a companywise meeting about to start, and you want to send out a quick reminder to the staff. IM is a neat way to do this.

Louderback—and other industry columnists—list a host of other benefits to IM, most relating back to the idea of immediacy and efficiency. In this process of rearticulation, journalists, programmers, and managers participate in the process of strengthening the tendential force on the idea of instanteous information transfer—the employee at the other end of the message is assumed to instantly respond to the management directive.

This rearticulation also requires a corresponding disarticulation—IM was initially blocked at many corporate sites not only because employees used it for off-task communication.[9] IM use was also articulated as a dangerous security hole. An earlier *eWeek* Lab's report on IM begins with this question-and-answer exchange (the question purportedly a "compelling and frequently asked question" at "a recent *eWeek* eSeminar on IM in the enterprise"):

> **IM technology is free today for all enterprises via any of the public IM networks. What is the justification for implementing gateways and an IM infrastructure?**
>
> It really comes down to control, security, and the ability to monitor, archive, and filter content. ("Labs Answers IM Questions" *eWeek*, April 14, 2003; bold original)

One might take the response as an ironic joke (it is difficult for me to read the response without it sounding like an attack on corporate control, but in this context it is meant to be delivered with a straight face), but the way in which IM has been articulated in corporations makes concerns about control—of communication, workers, technologies—paramount.[10] So the development of secure IM networks helps disarticulate the dangerous tendential force that constructs current and previous IM networks and clients. The rearticulation of IM, in these contexts, does not merely dismiss the technology or disable it. Instead the technology is taken up, rearticulated through a series of symbolic and material processes, and used in a different way. A rearticulated IM was deployed in 2003 in the U.S. invasion of Iraq to enable a "swarm theory" model for invasion (J. Davis, 2003). Online communication, ranging from IM to e-mail to chat rooms, was actively rearticulated in ways that strengthened some tendential forces (decentralized communication, increased efficiency). As a *Wired* article reports (in an article that manages to combine cynicism and geewhiz), troop movements are now structured on plans with concentric and overlapping circles rather than wedge-shaped linear vectors. The earlier model (used in the earlier U.S. invasion of Iraq) relied on line-of-site coordination among troops during movement. The wedge allowed drivers of vehicles to map their positions visually. This method worked, but required a larger number of vehicles and/or a smaller area of control because each vehicle needed to remain in constant visual contact with at least one other vehicle.

Rearticulations of communication technologies on board U.S. military vehicles, however, allow vehicles to remain in one-to-one communication even when not in view of each other. The swarm theory model

> holds that you move fast and don't worry about securing the rear. The benefits to this are many. First, you need fewer troops and less equipment. War becomes cheaper. Second, it's harder for the enemy to attack a widely dispersed formation. Third, units can cover much more ground—they aren't forced to maintain the wedge by slowing down to accommodate lagging vehicles. Fourth, swarming allows you to go straight for the heart of the enemies command structure, undermining its support from the inside out rather than battling on the periphery. (J. Davis, 2003, n.p.)

Yet articulations, at least strongly structured ones, are frequently difficult to change. Thus, although some attempts appear to be successful, the *Wired* article points to several incomplete or failing rearticulations. The *Wired* reporter, during a tour of a two-man missile delivery truck, begins surreptitiously experimenting with the computer system onboard the truck. The specialist in charge of the tour spots him.

> "It's pretty neat," says [Specialist] Fox. In the intensity of my discovery, I didn't notice him watching me. For a second, I worry that he'll slam the system shut. Instead, he shows me the chat application. He points to a horizontal window running across the top of the screen above the map. A few messages are visible, one highlighted in red.
>
> "This one's new," he says, double-clicking it.
>
> *Guess who?* it reads.
>
> *Is this Sergeant Lopez?* Fox types in.
>
> *No*, comes the reply.
>
> *Is it Sergeant Walker?*
>
> *No.*
>
> "What do you normally use the system for?" I ask, wondering about the use of my tax dollars.
>
> "Not much yet," he shrugs. "We just got it installed last week."

Fox goes on to provide a rearticulation in which batallions rely on chat to verify positions displayed on maps.

These complex and contingent processes of rearticulation illustrate freeplay within articulations as well as limits to rearticulation, both in terms of the concrete technologies and their symbolic value. In some contexts, IM is articulated by developers, users, and other participants as a disruptive, dangerous technology. In other contexts, IM is articulated as a highly efficient tool for corporate or military communication. The possibility of slippage in the system—like that in the system of language—is what allows technologies to be used in varying contexts. Yet that slippage is rarely completely free; completely fluid systems develop into schizophrenia.

In the remaining chapters, I extend the examination of information space articulations, moving from familiar to emerging technologies, as well as other media, to look for new ways of articulating information space as a contextually based, contingent construction.

Notes

1. Novelist Richard Powers ("Wired," 1999) used a similarly large interface on occasion, projecting a computer image onto a bedroom wall while he reclined in bed with a dictation headset, voice-recognition software, and a wireless keyboard.
2. From Digidesign's Web site, http://www.digidesign.com/ 1.19.02.
3. This practice is similar to Faber's need to "work with stuff," although Dies' creation of a palette is a more contingent act. The need to get information "out there," in a visible, interactive surface, and the desire to create a pool of potential pieces of information (information that the user is not sure he or she will actually need) seem to be features of emerging symbolic-analytic practices.
4. A tambre describes the attack/decay of a tone over time and its harmonic structure. Musicians refer to the temporal aspect of the tone as a *shape*, a linguistic move toward postmodernism, with time becoming spatialized to analyze and manipulate it. In chapter 5, I discuss Foucault's assertion in "Of Other Spaces" that postmodernism involves a shift away from history and toward space, with time becoming spatialized.
5. A fact pointed out by Clay Spinuzzi during a discussion of datacloud working environments.
6. As I discuss in a later chapter, Dies' creation of music from fragments echoes work by other musicians ranging from Steve Reich's and Philip Glass' avant garde looping music in the 1960s, the alternative band The Flaming Lips' use of prerecorded cassettes during concerts, and turntablists such as Cut Chemist's mixing of prerecorded LPs in performance.

7.   Indeed as Selber (2003) pointed out, even something as simple as drafting a report is much more complex than we often articulate it; we tend to focus on necessary, but functional, aspects of writing at the expense of more complex issues. If we want to teach writing and design as symbolic-analytic activities—and I think we must—then we have to come to terms with writing and design as complex activities requiring new pedagogies and practices.

.8   In fact the front portion of the lab offers a large, ceiling-mounted projection system used for teaching and technology training; this system is used collaboratively only with much effort and on rare occasions.

.9   This off-task criticism has been leveled at nearly every networked communication technology, including the telephone, e-mail, and the Web.

10.   There are contexts, such as financial services companies, in which such surveillance and archiving are legally mandated by the Securities and Exchange Commission (SEC), as the *eWeek* article points out. Yet those situations would seem to be the minority rather than the rule.

5

ARTICULATING (IN) THE DATACLOUD

Every great entrepreneur is both geek and shrink.
—R. Reich, (2001, p. 57)

You are going to have to operate your analysis of meaning without the solace of closure: more on the basis of the semantic raids that Benjamin proposed—to find the fragments, to decipher their assembly and see how you can make a surgical cut into them, assembling and reassembling the means and instruments of cultural production.
—Hall, (1989, p. 137)

Articulations are *suggestions* about acceptable meanings. Like language, they are ideological structures and processes that function most effectively when subjects act automatically following common sense. Ideologies *hail* us, to use Althusser's (1971) terms: They call us to act as subjects, and when we act on their authority, we typically fail to recognize ideologies as constructs, but instead treat them as natural conditions and decisions.

In her extended analysis of the telephone, for example, Ronell (1989) pointed out the ways in which a ringing telephone calls us—In hearing the ring, we recognize ourselves as the subject who must answer, a calling that is simultaneously auditory and ideological.

> . . . And yet, you're saying yes, almost automatically, suddenly, sometimes irreversibly. Your picking it up means the call has come through. It means more: you're its beneficiary, rising to meet its demand, to pay a debt. You don't know who's calling or what you are going to be called upon to do, and still, you are lending your ear, giving something up, receiving an order. It is a question of answerability. Who answers the call of the telephone, the call of duty, and accounts for the taxes it appears to impose? (Ronell, 1989, p. 2)

In most cases we do not even know what other person might be on the line,[1] but nonetheless we recognize the need to answer.[2] This seems natural to us most of the time—common sense. Yet the artificiality of that calling is made apparent to anyone who has stood at the counter of a store, discussing a purchase with a clerk, when the phone behind the counter rang. As customers, the interruption appeared to be just that—a break-down in the process of commerce. Yet from the clerk's subject position, the ringing phone hailed him or her, called on him or her to answer. To our growing annoyance, the clerk raised the handset and entered a separate space of discourse, offering, "How may I help you?" That *you* was once us, but now became someone else's *you*. The clerk was recruited into an artic-ulation from which we are abruptly pushed away. And so ideologies go: When they work, they seem natural and unavoidable.

The task of changing articulations and ideologies is extremely difficult: Protesting their actions often marks us as rude and disruptive. Indeed changing articulations—disarticulating and rearticulating them—requires disruption. Ideologies are, by definition, arrangements that tend to run smoothly. They are literally necessary to everyday life it seems. We cannot go about grappling with infinite possible meanings for every potential action we encounter or we would never get anywhere.

Schizophrenia—the condition of postmodernism according to Deleuze and Guattari (1987)—describes the inability to filter input. So all of us rely on assumptions about ideological structures, consciously or not, on strong tendential forces to understand what it means to work and learn.

In general this works pretty well. Do not let any theorist tell you oth-erwise. Occasionally, however, articulations begin to unravel—to shift or be shifted, sometimes due to our conscious efforts, sometimes against our better judgment, sometimes without our even noticing, sometimes all three. The case of Instant Messenger (IM) is a useful example to return to, because it encapsulates a moment in which all three tendencies appear (Fig. 5.1).

The decision to include IM software on lab computers, described early in this text, was partially my own. It was clear students used the applica-tion extensively: An application timelog that runs on our networks showed AOL IM to be the number one application in use in the lab. Not coinciden-tally, IM is in heavy use because many students launch the program and log in nearly any time they are working. They are not actively using IM during that period, but have it open, off in a corner of the screen, sometimes hid-den by other windows. They are, routinely, always already in IM no matter what else they are doing. In effect, IM is a constant feature of their com-puter use.

Fig. 5.1. Buddy list in iChat, an IM client.

The program, therefore, is not necessarily in *active* use for the sheer number of hours that other programs (like Microsoft Word or Dreamweaver) might be. Yet because IM surfaces periodically, over and over again, for many people it punctuates their working and learning lives in an unusual way. From my own frame of reference, the messages that students send and receive during class are distracting and somewhat rude.

I also have to question whether my method of working and learning is necessarily the best or most appropriate to the overall or even local goals unless the primary goal of students is to meet my expectations, which it is not. Yet the decision to install the program was one I made in consultation with the students who staff the lab when we configured the machines.

I have to admit that I expected some degree of in-class, off-topic use, but I did not anticipate how prevalent messaging would become in class. This rearticulation of what sorts of activities were appropriate in class, then, is in one respect a conscious decision, and in another sense something I found myself resisting.

Only later did it occur to me that the program was part of a more general rearticulation, one connected up, network fashion, to cultural shifts in the structures of learning and working. Eventually I came to understand IM in my class as unavoidable and sometimes even positive.

When I began teaching in the last decade of the 20th century, I originally thought of myself as the stereotypical college professor, envisioning myself as the lecturer at the front of the room espousing important theories and methods, which my students (in my naive imagination) would dutifully transport into their brains to guide them on their forays into the world of elegant prose. I was surprised to discover, during the pedagogy courses I took in preparation for teaching, that such notions had been replaced with models based on mentoring, coaching, and student-centered classrooms that focused on discussion, negotiation, and interaction.

So IM began to seem like one more way in which students engage in purposeful discourse, one other communication space that existed alongside, or even within, the space of the classroom. The structure of my classes began to change as I recognized that my insistence on sustained attention to the man talking in the front of the room did not facilitate the forms of learning that I was espousing. Lecture material was increasingly moved to out-of-class readings or compacted into short mini-lectures designed to cover specific topics as needed. Although someone situated in a traditional worldview might find such structures chaotic, these structures more closely matched the forms of learning and work appropriate to symbolic-analytic work.

SM:[3]	humm, yeah i was on the phone, lol the chem hw is not to bad, most of it we learned last lec
EM:	(which I missed)
SM:	monday u missed?
EM:	yea
EM:	and friday
SM:	u get the notes off line?
EM:	and today
EM:	not yet but I will
EM:	chemistry is the easiest subject for me
SM:	yeah like it is easy to understand
EM:	yea it's lewis structures
SM:	yeah and some humm like formal charges
EM:	not difficult
EM:	too bad we have two tests next week
SM:	yeah yeah that is goin to be a crazy times
SM:	lol i hate chem:-[
EM:	I like chem
EM:	I'll help you if you want
SM:	physics, humm fun fun, thanks:-D

SM: u got all that hw due tomorrow?
EM: what?
EM: I got to do some calc... so I'll ttyl
SM: u said u were doin calc
SM: lol
EM: I will be
EM: Adam's here.
SM: ok ttyl, have fun
EM: bye
SM: kk bye

The communication technologies I have discussed in this book all represent tendential forces that disrupt traditional notions of working and learning. Just as IM interrupts the primary focus of attention in the classroom, MOO spaces make control of a classroom difficult to maintain in the conventional sense. Newcomers to MOO are often overwhelmed by the necessity of filtering multiple, nearly simultaneous real-time conversations going on in a single window. In MOO classes and meetings I have attended, I often find myself tracking three or four concurrent discussion threads, each with different participants entwined with each other in the same scrolling window.

> D eena says, "How do you get people interested in the immersive and the material? in the dialogue possibilities inherent in the MOOs?"
> D eena2 has been peeking at the stray questions on the right hand side.
> Dene says, "not everyone does, Deena"
> Salmon [to Deena]: good question.. and i think that's one thing we're trying to answer with poetrix
> Dene says, "some people are not comnfortable with the switch"
> Helen says, "Newcomers often just play around being "silly" - only some of them ever go on to create more interesting things"
> D eena says, "Salmon I missed poetrix. Is there a URL?""
> MazThing bridles at the concept that silly isn't serious too.
>   cahoots sides with maz
> Dene says, "this MOO is a web"
> Salmon says, "poetrix is very much in development, so i'll give you a URL, but recommend that you don't visit until after the chat, k?"
> Salmon says, "things are, borky, as we say.."

D eena says, "Sure, I am on shaky ground here as it is...want stuff for
    later reading."

Helen thinks there is silly and silly: some newbies never get the point
    that this is "real"

Salmon says, "http://poetrix.net"

D eena wonders what borky is.

D eena says, "Helen, Salmon, Dene, all, what do we mean by real
    here?"

Dryad agrees that silly and play are important...and perhaps more useful in teaching the possibilities of a MOO than introducing it as a
chat room or an archive.

Helen says, "Bookmark poetrix to visit later...."

Dene says, "that it is happening?"

MazThing [to Helen]: well, it *is* and it *isn't* real. MOOs are about
    consensual text....it is what you make it, whatever the originator
    meant.

Salmon says, "isn't really interested in questions about what is real"

Salmon isn't either :0

Dene nods

Dryad [to MazThing]: I very much like that notion of "consensual text".

Salmon agress with dryad

Sue says, "sometimes the issue is not to make out how much fun it is,
    but how serious it can be"

D eena says, "How do you teach the possiblities of a MOO? What do
    students get out of these possibilities?"

Dryad [to MazThing]: both as consenting (agreeing) and as "feeling
    together"...if I may play with the word.

Helen invites everyone to contribute if they have something to say:
    later we will tour MOO spaces

(Nouspsace session log at
http://trace.ntu.ac.uk/forumlive/chat022003.cfm)

To newcomers, the sensation is something like being at a frat party in
which every conversation occurs at top volume. I wondered why the
designers of these spaces had not come up with interface methods for sorting out conversation threads similar to the way newgroup readers allow col-
lapsing and expanding single discussions thread by thread rather than forcing the user to read all at once.

Eventually, I realized that this was one of the *benefits* of the MOO
interface—rather than a single conversation, I had a small datacloud, a rel-

atively unstructured mass of conversation in which multiple conversations occurred on the same general plane. Like most users, I developed skills at navigating this space—of not only sorting out the various threads, but also of seeing these as not three, four, or $n+$ separate threads, but often as aspects of the same conversation.

During one class several years ago, my department chair sat in the back of the room while I and 15 PhD students in a seminar sat in front of our keyboards typing madly away, interacting with each other in our MOOspace. The only sound in the room was the clattering of keyboards interspersed with muffled laughs and periodic interjections of "Yes!" and "Ha!" as participants in the onscreen conversation grappled with the readings assigned for that week. The department chair sat in front of a blank computer screen—I had failed to tell him to login and participate in the discussion. His facial expression varied between detached bemusement and confusion.

None of this is remarkable; I offer it primarily as another example of a feature that appears to be a design flaw, but instead comes to be a benefit. As the old (but still relevant) programmer's joke goes, "That's not a bug! It's a feature!" Like all good jokes, it contains a grain of truth.

As information spaces, MOO and IM operate in different ways. MOOs tend toward reaffirming real-world spatial and temporal relations because of the demands they make on users (both in time and screen real estate). Although working in a MOO does not require the same order of presence required in face-to-face conversation, community membership tends to require participants to maintain personae over time, put forth efforts to build spaces in the MOO, and participate actively. In fact, MOOs are communities for some people at least as strong as (and sometimes stronger than) available face-to-face communities. IM sessions, conversely, are sporadic and fragmented. They take place in relatively small and narrow windows, encourage brief exchanges, and occur (in general) in smaller spaces (both conceptually and spatially).

Despite the common complaint (by teachers, parents, and others) that IM sessions are disruptive, the situation is actually much different for experienced users of the technology, both in classrooms and corporate spaces. As Issacs (2003) reported on research at AT&T Labs,

> [F]our colleagues and I had the opportunity to study a very large sample of monitored IM interactions—over 21,000 IM conversations involving 437 users conducted from mid-2000 to late 2001. . . .
>
> Our study suggests that some people seem to be very effective at discussing complex work topics using nothing more than text. And since all users often multitask while engaged in IM conversations, it would be

a mistake to tightly integrate IM with certain applications, thereby making it difficult for users to jump from one application to another.

Our results also suggest that the characteristics of heavy IM use—multiple, brief, intermittent interactions throughout the day whereby the lines of communication are more or less left open for spontaneous conversation—mirror the nature of impromptu pair-wise interactions in other media. This finding suggests that other tools intended to supplement or work with IM should seek to support the characteristics of the sort of lightweight, unplanned interactions we witness each day in the places we work.

These sorts of experiences are similar to the ones of students whom I have surveyed, who tended to use IM for a wide range of activities—socializing composed a large portion, but students also used the technology for class meetings, locating resources for homework, coordinating team projects, and more. In a short Web-based survey that I posed in the fall of 2003, 450 users (primarily college students at the graduate and undergraduate levels) described their use of IM. Most survey respondents to the survey were attending my own university, although students and faculty from other schools responded as well.[4]

This self-selected group was dominated by relatively young (average age 20.5 years), high-tech users: Their academic majors or career paths tended heavily toward engineering (more than 50%) and computing (16%). They were predominantly (close to 75%) male, to some extent reflecting the unbalanced male to female ratio at the university where I work, but possibly also reflecting gendered differences in willingness to respond to technical questions.

The respondents claimed a large number of IM sessions per day—the average was more than 15 sessions, with several respondents indicating 20, 30, or 50 sessions per day. They also appeared to be able to prioritize tasks—when asked whether they ignored IM requests when they were busy, more than half indicated that they routinely or always did. Fewer than 10% said they never or rarely ignored IM requests when they were busy.

This survey was obviously not exhaustive and is more suggestive than explanatory (let alone scientific). Yet it does provide a fairly coherent picture of the potential for these fragmented technologies to emerge in powerful ways within educational and work spaces. When I ask students in my class to select their preferred medium—cell phone, e-mail, or IM—for casual communication with friends, IM wins by an enormous margin (sometimes unanimously in a class).

User 1 : what are you doing tonight?
User 2 : doing some work then probably just watching tv
User 2 : I got to do some stuff for the house too
User 1 : are you going to be in your room around 11?
User 2 : I should be
User 1 : you have a book on html right?
User 2 : yeah
User 1 : do you mind if I borrow it?
User 2 : No, but I might need it back later this week
User 1 : yeah that's fine. I'll get it around 11
User 2 : ok, later
User 1 : later

As Isaacs indicated, the ubiquitous nature of IM allows it to emerge in the spaces between other forms of work; its fragmentation is a strength in many situations rather than a weakness or distraction. The growing importance of such fragmentation is associated with new approaches to education and work emerging in our cultures.

TENDENTIAL FORCES IN EDUCATION AND WORK

As I discussed earlier in relation to the history of interface design, computer interfaces have shifted to support different forms of working and learning over the last five or six decades. In addition to the shifts in the location and type of learning related to computers, they also now provide an enormous range of facilities for manipulating, filtering, sorting, and transforming preexisting information—a development that allowed (and perhaps encouraged) the development of the job classification of symbolic-analytic work.

The rise of symbolic-analytic work and environments in which that work takes place has not, however, been matched by the development of an educational system designed for teaching these skills. In many cases, students are actively discouraged from learning symbolic-analytic skills. For example, although students frequently learn generalized research skills, too little attention is paid to working with masses of information. As information scientist Mirel (1996) pointed out, learning how to work with databases too frequently prioritizes technical functionality over constructing effective communications:

> [D]ata reporting is a rhetorical action that is rarely taught in technical
> and professional writing classes. Instead, if people at work formally
> learn about data reporting at all, it is in computer training courses,
> which teach users how to execute data retrieval and reporting func-
> tions. This training stresses technological over rhetorical skills and
> knowledge, mistakenly assuming that knowing how to operate a tech-
> nology is commensurate with knowing how to use it to its full advan-
> tage to achieve a purposeful exchange of information. (pp. 92–93)

In her study, Mirel interviewed project administrators at a national lab-
oratory who used data reports to assess financial activity in their area of
responsibility. The reports, generated by IS staff, can be read in the structure determined by the IS staff or interactively restructured using a second
computer program. Administrators were uniformly unhappy with the
reports in the default format, saying that the data they were given made it
difficult to answer the four key questions the report was supposed to help
them answer (simple questions such as "What is the difference between
budgeted and actual costs?").

Despite this dissatisfaction, only 3 out of 25 administrators used the
supplied computer program to revise the data report so that it provided the
data in a useful format. Five administrators manually rekeyed data into
another database to rearrange data. The other 17 apparently made do with
the inappropriately structured data.

Mirel's research applies to the problem of educating articulation workers in two ways. First, the IS staff who created the reports failed to config-
ure data in ways that would connect up with the ongoing needs of the users
of those data. Second, the scientists in general possessed the administra-
tive and traditional communication skills necessary for evaluating data, but
lacked the additional information manipulation skills necessary for working in and with the information in any form beyond that in which they
received it.

Similarly, Spinuzzi's (2003) research on workers analyzing traffic accident data in Iowa demonstrated the ways in which users struggle to represent and use information in meaningful ways. Spinuzzi's users were somewhat more successful in learning to modify the system in successive ways
to create more useful representations. Communication breakdowns sometimes resulted in improvements in the system from a symbolic-analytic
point of view.

Nearly every type of symbolic-analytic or articulation work requires
the ability to work at an advanced level with information spaces such as
this. Unfortunately, formal education often fails to provide the complex

environments necessary to teach students these skills, for several related reasons. Even in common programs students do not use many of the robust information work tools provided; their articulation of work in these contexts tends toward routine production rather than symbolic-analytic work. Brasseur (1994) documented the tendency of students to accept default settings in Excel-generated graphics, even when those settings damage the rhetorical purpose of the graphic. Tufte's (2003) attacks on PowerPoint as a presentation technology decry the ubiquitous use of the program (see Fig. 5.2), likening it to a

> widely used and expensive prescription drug . . . with frequent, serious side effects: It induced stupidity, turned everyone into bores, wasted time, and degraded the quality and credibility of communication.
>
> In a business setting, a PowerPoint slide typically shows 40 words, which is about eight seconds' worth of silent reading material. With so little information per slide, many, many slides are needed. Audiences consequently endure a relentless sequentiality, one damn slide after another. When information is stacked in time, it is difficult to understand context and evaluate relationships. Visual reasoning usually works more effectively when relevant information is shown side by side. Often, the more intense the detail, the greater the clarity and understanding. This is especially so for statistical data, where the fundamental analytical act is to make comparisons.

I would be the first to argue with the observation that PowerPoint is frequently a strong tendential force articulating execrable presentations. Yet other articulations are certainly possible. Byrne's (2003) response to Tufte (see Fig. 5.3), for example, rearticulated PowerPoint and technology in general in critical ways:

> In thinking about graphic design, industrial design, and what might really be the cutting-edge of design, I realized it would have to be genetic engineering. Dolly (God rest her soul) represents the latest in design, but it is, in her case, design we cannot see. Dolly looks like any other sheep, which is precisely the point. The dogma of some graphic designers is that their work be invisible. This perfection has been achieved with Dolly.

Although interfaces, along with social contexts and other forces, tend to articulate linear, difficult to analyze communications as Tufte charges, this should not be surprising given that users are not encouraged to do otherwise, either by the software or context they are in.

Fig. 5.2. Graphic from Tufte's "The Cognitive Style of PowerPoint".

Fig. 5.3. PowerPoint slide by David Byrne.

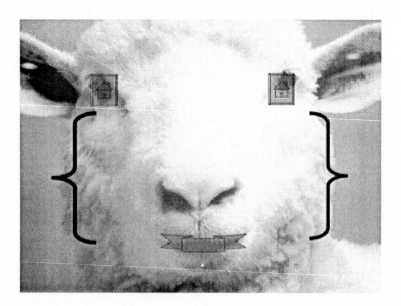

In such contexts, users, tend to apply a process of trial-and-error to achieve minimally acceptable results within one application, but have little experience learning a new system, let alone advancing their learning beyond the novice level. Sometimes (too often), students do not learn to understand that information is not neutral, but needs to be looked at critically, challenged, and transformed—*used* rather than simply *received*.

In addition, software in general still fails to support information work in robust ways: In many programs, information is either something users *consume* or *produce*; there is little room for transformative consumption, advanced filtering, or hybrid consumption/production that would lie at the heart of symbolic-analytic work, let alone a practice of articulation that possessed both a cognitive and material, visible aspect.

This imbalance shows up when we map software according to its support for work in two philosophical and material dimensions: working in time and working in space. A major component of the power of articulation theory and practice lies in its ability to work productively within postmodernist spaces. In at least one way of seeing the move from modernist to postmodernist culture (one suggested by Foucault and Lyotard, among others) inheres in the loss of history as an organizing feature to both cultural and quotidian existence.

> The great obsession of the nineteenth century was, as we know, history: with its themes of development and of suspension, of crisis and cycle, themes of the ever-accumulating past, with its great preponderance of dead men and the menacing glaciation of the world. The nineteenth century found its essential mythological resources in the second principle of thermodynamics. The present epoch will perhaps be above all the epoch of space. We are in the epoch of simultaneity: we are in the epoch of juxtaposition, the epoch of the near and the far, of the side-by-side, of the dispersed. We are at the moment, I believe, when our experience of the world is less that of a long life developing through time than that of a network that connects points and intersects with its own skein. One could perhaps say that certain ideological conflicts animating present-day polemics oppose the pious descendants of time and the determined inhabitants of space. (Foucault, 1986, p. 23)

Recall the analysis of David Dies' work in ProTools (chap. 4), and the creation of palettes of possible sounds in his composition, as well as my discussion of the musical concept of tambre, which refers to temporal aspects (attack/decay) in spatial forms. Urban planner and social theorist Paul Virilio (1997) similarly noted that contemporary cultures are primarily involved in the control of space.

Articulation theory, as Hall (1983) constructed it, aims to mediate between history and space without either falling back into a simple, deterministic historical narrative or degenerating into pure fragmentation. The processes of articulation (disarticulation and rearticulation) involve both historical and spatial aspects: Nothing is predetermined by historical weight (as Hall said, articulation is "marxism without guarantees"), but history still matters—it provides tendential force.

Most office productivity software remains tied to a relatively orderly modernist vision of information use: orderly, discrete, objective, and knowable. Yet in a postmodernist era, the loss of a grand, organizing narrative (ultimate goals or beginnings) removes the rudder guiding modernist labor. Workers move in short, linear bursts—writing memos and TPS reports; reading short pages on the Web, watching animations and short films. In many interpretations, the short, linked bursts of linear activity are mistakenly labeled *spatial* or *hypertextual*, although they remain ordered by linear time rather than space (a jagged line is multidimensional only to the extent that the line branches, recurses, and covers space rather than just proceeds forward).

In interfaces that relate to information work, we begin to see a split: Programs that support information *consumption* tend to prioritize the line and time, whereas those that support information *production* tend to prioritize space (and often colonize time by turning it into space). Some programs support both information production and consumption, with a small class (which I return to later) supporting production and consumption as both temporal and spatial activities—in other words, disarticulation and rearticulation. These activities suggest new directions for support for symbolic-analytic work.

In the popular information space of the Web, for example, consumption and production most frequently occur in separate programs. Internet Explorer (Fig. 5.4) supports, most prominently, moving forward or backward in lines.[5]

Although we commonly insist that the hypertextual organization of the Web suggests reading a network rather than a linear text, the experience of reading the Web for most users remains that of following a line. The temporal experience of page to page to page anchors the reading experiences in history, even a fragmented and abbreviated one. As such, most Web use remains tied to the consumption of time. Compare this interface to those in more advanced Web development interfaces, where users are articulated as information workers in more spatial environment (see Fig. 5.5).

In general, then, information-consumption and information-production environments tend to be separated. Consumption environments tend

Fig. 5.4. Internet Explorer.

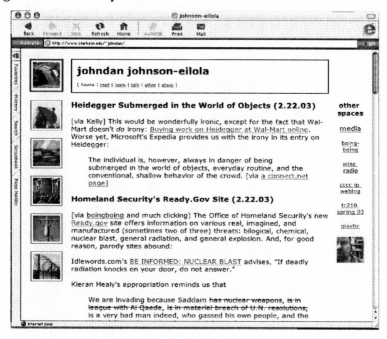

Fig. 5.5. Dreamweaver interface.

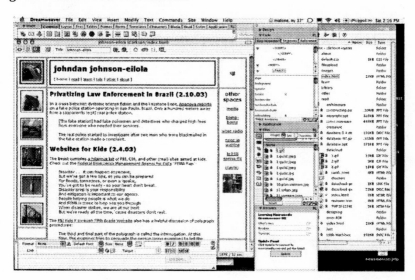

to support work along the temporal axis, whereas, information production tends toward more spatial aspects even when considering the same media.

The graph in Fig. 5.6 shows shifts in the contexts of production and contexts of use for various media and genres. Those shifts are obviously generic and depend, in great part, on specific, concrete uses. What I am suggesting here, however, is the current general articulation of consumption as much less spatial than the current general articulation of production. In other words, people who produce media are articulated in more spatial ways than people who consume the same media. Some media or genres typically use the same interface for both production and consumption (e-mail, IM): These tend to prioritize neither time nor space and are somewhat fragmented, allowing them to be integrated into other contexts relatively easily.

Fig. 5.6. Map of information production and use for various media. Arrows point from production emphasis to consumption emphasis. Media without arrows are both produced and consumed in relatively similar environments.

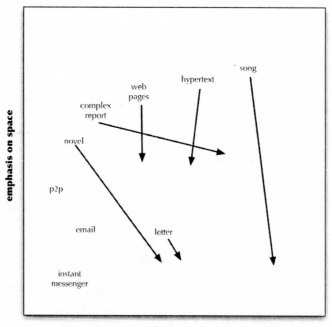

Still, although this map is suggestive, we also need to consider the more complex acts of production and use. For example, the development of a complex report is generally a spatial activity (especially if we conceive of that report in ways articulated by and as symbolic-analytic work). Such a project might entail large masses of notes in various media (physical and virtual), quotations, outlines, commentaries from others, graphics, photocopied pages, bookmarks in a Web browser, and numerous other resources and media. In this sense, the production of the report would be spatial (consider information flow in Brent Faber's office in chap. 4, which is an early example of such work). Yet the production environment for the report—frequently a word-processing application such as Microsoft Word—is extremely linear and temporal and aimed at linear texts.

Although Microsoft has surfaced a great deal of information about producing texts, at least at the functional level (and has begun to integrate Web-authoring capabilities), Word's overall orientation remains tied to simple linear texts—and to the idea that texts are authored by individuals rather than assembled from fragments: Although the program can import chunks of information such as the movie still image in Fig. 5.7, manipulating that image remains awkward—oriented around resizing and touching up, not filtering, dis- and reconnecting, or other symbolic-analytic activities.

Fig. 5.7. Word interface.

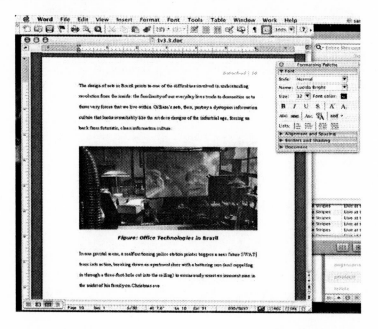

Still the support of work within information spaces—symbolic-analytic work or articulation practice—remains tentative even in Web-authoring programs such as Dreamweaver. Although the program provides libraries of commonly used files, a catalogue of existing (and planned) pages on a particular Web site, and more, robust information work requires support not merely for *production*, but for the recursive acts of *production* and *consumption*. Hence Dreamweaver continues to submerge the activities of research, browsing the Web, taking notes, and making connections to the work of others in active and critical ways.

Notes

1. Caller ID may be changing this situation (at home I rarely answer the phone if I do not recognize the number originating the call). Still for the purposes of understanding ideological hailing, the telephone acts as a useful example even if it must be placed in a historical context.
2. During meetings with students and colleagues in my office, I often let the phone ring, unanswered, to continue an important conversation. I have discovered, however, that most people are unable to hold a conversation in the presence of a ringing phone. The volume of the ring is not so loud as to disrupt conversation, but the ideological hailing is difficult to ignore.
3. I've changed the screen names here to protect the identity of the users.
4. I did not track IP numbers or require respondents to identify themselves. Respondents could volunteer their name, location, and e-mail address if they wished to be considered for a follow-up question. The majority of, but not all, respondents who provided this information were from my own institution.
5. An interesting exception is the use of a History menu in most browsers, which records and captures the linear series of pages viewed, allowing users to skip forward and backward in relatively nonlinear ways.

6

OTHER STORIES, OTHER TEXTS: OTHER IDEAS ABOUT WORK

Music is an art. It appeals to our senses. Music is also a language. It's a symbol system. We have traditionally privileged texts as our primary rhetorical medium. Should we rethink this? According to Kenneth Burke, the poetic and the rhetorical are all the same. Both art and argument ask an audience to identify with the intention of the speaker. If we can accept Burke's argument, and if we can accept that symbolic actions transcend what we would usually regard as language, then we need to reconsider not only visual media, but also auditory media in rhetorical acts. Music asks an audience to do more than feel. It asks an audience to accept or reject certain social memberships. And it asks an audience to make sense of those relationships that it evokes. . . .

Music resides in the provenance of composition by virtue of rhetoric.

—Taylor and Halbritter (2003)

You are children, playing a game, but nonetheless a master of eloquence. Your success at the game depends on your persuasive ardor as much as your ability. Positions and figures in space are the power of rhetoric.

The same holds true for the novice or the expert. Such is the teaching of Menander of Laodicea, known as Rhetor, in his exhortations in praise of cities.

—Koolhaas et al. (2001, p. 23)

One of the difficulties of contemporary software design lies in assumptions made about the type of work users are doing. These assumptions are not necessarily incorrect because many (perhaps most) users still require tools for relatively straightforward tasks: producing simple linear texts for print, passively reading Web sites, or playing solitaire. In these contexts, it makes

sense for work to be articulated as a process of simple production and consumption; it makes sense for interfaces to be articulated as relatively closed
spaces. Yet for symbolic-analytic work of the type I have described, and for
the workers who I have been observed, different approaches are needed.
Communication and work are no longer simple, and people within these
spaces are no longer crying out for simplicity. Instead they require complexity, both in content and structure; they require contingency; and they
require movement.

Before examining some interfaces that begin to support these new
forms of work (which I take up in a subsequent chapter), I am going to take
a brief detour through two fields that might inform an analysis (and extension). The first, music, offers some useful suggestions about ways that texts
might be broken down and reused, as well as ways that text becomes contingent, collaborative performance in space rather than static, isolated artifact. The second field I examine, deconstructivist architecture, informs a
critique of current information architecture, the interdisciplinary practice of
designing information. Although information architecture is an invaluable
aspect of interface design, I demonstrate ways that its emphasis on simplicity and transparency often limits the usefulness of designed spaces for
symbolic-analytic work.

CUTS, CHANNELS, AND LOOPS: REARTICULATING MUSIC

What this is all about is the art of mixing. It's analog . . . It's right in
front of you. They don't need a delay line: they're creating delays with
beat juggling or in moving the fader in certain ways to stagger things
and to stutter things and to manipulate time with your hands.
—Humon (cited in Blondheim, Meza, & Pray, 2001)

We're not sure what to call it yet, so we've been using the term "experimental concerts" or "boom-box experiment", anyway, something
that, hopefully, implies a work in progress. What will be happening
tonight is similar to the "parking lot experiments" in that what you'll
be hearing are pre-recorded tapes. But, instead of being in car stereos,
tonight's performance uses hand held boom boxes, forty of them,
using volunteers from the audience to engage and manipulate each

separate sound source. Wayne and Steven will be guiding the manipulation of the boom boxes and Michael is the center monitor source. This is the first time these compositions will be heard by both the audience and the creators..So, we hope it goes well and we hope you like it. As we are still skeptical about its "entertainment" value. . . .
—The Flaming Lips, *Boombox No. 13 Handout*

Most contemporary interfaces do not provide us with the sorts of tools necessary to create spaces for symbolic-analytic work. Perhaps just as important, our social contexts still tend to articulate information work as the quest for simplicity and clarity.

Symbolic-analytic work, however, relies on the activity (technically and conceptually) of manipulating massive amounts of disparate information, combining elements of different types, and testing new structures and processes. Current interfaces cannot contain enough information. Thus, as we saw in the case of the complex work done by Faber and Dies (and alluded to by McDougall), information often must be maintained outside of the interface—moved into and out of the interface manually.

I want to take a brief detour here—a musical interlude—to explore some alternative ways of understanding information work as symbolic-analytic, with creativity articulated not as the creation of unique information in a vacuum, but as involving the manipulation of preexisting pieces of information in space. I consider two related musical events or movements. First, I discuss the ways that turntablism—scratching—implicitly addresses the symbolic-analytic work issue as a way to orchestrate temporal fragments, constructing a timeline from heterogeneous, disjointed spaces. Second, I turn to work done by The Flaming Lips that constructs music as a collaborative, contingent, spatial experience. These two articulations of communication and technology suggest interesting ways that we can consider pushing interfaces that support symbolic-analytic work (as well as symbolic-analytic work).

Verse 1: Turntablism and the Breakdown and Re-Orchestration of Time

Rap, hip-hop, and turntablism, in general, have long understood culture in a profoundly postmodern way—a constant process or dis- and rearticulation. Unlike many postmodern practices, however, these forms of music are not about merely cutting up the past, but re-using history in ways that are by turns respectful, playful, active, productive, and perhaps worthy of extended study and learning. Such attitudes (increasingly prevalent many forms of contemporary music) highlight and strengthen the connections between music consumption (often considered a primarily passive activity) and music production.

Turntablism involves a highly developed form of what was once called *scratching*—the back-and-forth movement of a needle on a vinyl album to create rhythmic, recursive loops, often played between two turntables hooked to a fader that allowed instrumental breaks in songs to be extended indefinitely. Turntablists have added to these foundational skills a much larger and more finely developed repertoire of techniques to realize the turntable as a fully fledged musical instrument rather than simply a playback device.

Key to understanding turntablism is the notion that the DJ is a creative agent articulating new meanings by creatively mixing fragments of preexisting information. Plasticman explained,

> The easiest thing in the world is to just play back the data. The harder thing is to modify the data and make it work with other things by using EQ or effects. You can decide which data to cross over between the two sources. That's where it becomes a musical art form. (cited in Reighley, 2001, p. 116)

Traditional musicians (and traditionalists in general) downplay the creativity involved in turtablism because the notes are pre-recorded. One might argue, that many valued musical instruments rely on essentially pre-recorded or preconfigured instruments. Pianos and guitars, for example, are both structured as spatial sets of pretuned notes that are "played back" by striking keys or plucking strings. Yet this argument misses the point: In a postmodernist era, creativity is about movement, connection, and selection rather than a mythical genius ability to pull inspiration from within.

DJs are conscious of the differential status accorded to turntables by the public and some other musicians. As Rob Swift argued,

> The turntable is a musical instrument as long as you can see it being a musical instrument. You're dealing with notes, you're dealing with measures, you're dealing with timing, you're dealing with rhythm. It's just, you know, different tools, but the outcome is the same: music. (cited in Blondheim et al., 2001)

Although some aspects of turntablism are obvious to even casual listeners, as with other forms of advanced work, understanding the complexity of DJing is not automatic, but a learned or experienced thing.

> I have like a traditional music upbringing. I was always in a band. I played the piano and drums. I started drums when I was seven and just all through high school, marching band, snare drum. I can read music. I played trumpet. But with scratching, I just heard the "wikka-wikka" you know, like really easy, simple stuff and I was like, anyone can do that. But then I saw him and he's like doing all these crazy tricks and all these patterns that somehow I can't even play on the drums. And I was like, Oh my gosh, I've got to learn how to do that. (DJ Shortee; cited in Blondheim et al., 2001)

As DJ Shortee suggests (see Fig. 6.1), articulating turntablism as a musical form involves constructing parallels between turntables and more traditional instruments. In fact from a symbolic-analytic perspective, the piano might be considered a rudimentary instrument in comparison to a pair of Technics 1200 turntables and a nearly infinite field of music to draw on: A piano sports only 88 keys, each normally tuned to a single note. One

Fig. 6.1. DJ Shortee < http://www.faustandshortee.com >

cannot import new sounds (apart from the painstaking process of configuring a prepared piano or a sampling keyboard, which emulates turntablism). Creativity with such technology occupies a small space of possibilities. Yet creativity in the era of symbolic-analytic work offers new environments for work and much richer and more dynamic technological support.

As with all symbolic-analytic work, turntablism requires advanced skills in searching for information, breaking bodies of information apart, and recombining disparate pieces of information. DJs build personal archives of music to use as a resource (Fig. 6.2) by *digging*—combing through record stores for obscure music suitable for dropping into a set.

Fig. 6.2. Jazzy Jay showing a portion of his 3000,000 + album archive (Blondheim, Mesa, & Pray, 2001).

Digging provides DJs with the material for their sets. The ability to drop interesting cuts into a mix or juxtapose two different samples in interesting ways relies on building their repertoire. DJs frequently cover the labels of albums to prevent other DJs from knowing what obscure cuts they have played; others will tear pages out of phone books at pay phones to prevent other DJs from finding used record stores. DJ Shadow (see Fig. 6.3), for example, discusses spending years building a relationship with a record store to gain access to the massive storehouse of albums in basement storage.

Fig. 6.3. DJ Shadow, digging (Blondheim, Mesa, & Pray, 2001).

This is just . . . it's my little nirvana. Being a DJ, I take the art of digging seriously. And this [record store] is just a place I've been going to for eleven years. It's just an incredible archive of music culture. And there's the promise in these stacks of finding something that you're gonna use. And in fact, most of my first album is built off of records pulled from here. . . .

People that don't [dig]. You don't have to. It's not going to make a bad DJ good. But it'll make a good DJ better. (cited in Blondheim et al., 2001)

Although digging forms one component of the repertoire available to a skilled DJ, more important is the ability to juxtapose separate cuts in interesting ways, either serially or simultaneously.

Steinski: I remember going to see Afrikaa Bambatta, Planet Rock. [His DJ] Jazzy Jay was so funky. It was great. Moving from one break to the next, cutting two records together. It was just wonderful. Bambatta would be, you know, looking at the crowd, being this inscrutable master of records. . . .

At one point [Bambatta] took out a 45, slips it over Jazzy Jay's shoulder. And Jazz Jay looks up, takes it.[1]

Jazzy Jay: Bam would point to the line. Play the second cut. Play the second cut. The break is right there.

Steinski: Puts on the 45. And this break comes to the end and then, voop, voop, voop—lets it go. I was sitting there, and I was like, "Wait a minute. What?"

And it was the opening break from the Shirley Ellis record, "The Clapping Song." Which, I think the last time I heard it I was nine. And I really *liked* it when I was nine. And all of a sudden, everyone's dancing to this funky break. And I thought, that's fucking amazing. Afrikaa Bambatta: Master of records. (cited in Blondheim et al., 2001)

These skills—digging, mixing, and programming—represent an emerging space for symbolic-analytic work, one richer than most of us experience on a daily basis. Turntablism oscillates between temporal and spatial modes. To recall Foucault's opposition between modernism and postmodernism, DJs know history, but see it as a space for reuse—a storehouse. DJs alternate between *mix* and *program*.

Mixing focuses on transitions between cuts. Rob Swift explained,

There are certain laws and physics to the art of DJing that we all respond to and live by. You've got to know how to match two records, how to blend, and that will give you a sense of tempo, of speed. (cited in Reighley, 2000, p. 105)

Program focuses on the semantic relations among cuts. The early and influential album, *The Adventures of Grandmaster Flash on the Wheels of Steel* (1981), constructed an audio collage that included cuts from The Sugar Hill Gang, Blondie, Queen, Chic, Sequence and Soonie G, Furious Five, old Flash Gordon Radio Show archives, and an unnamed comedy record (Reighley, 2000).

Such collage work has begun appearing outside of the music world, as suggested by the quote from Taylor and Halbritter that opened this chapter. Taylor and Halbritter's work occurred as a performance at the Conference on College Composition and Communication, an annual event in which the presentation format typically involves the reading of papers and the display of slides via transparencies or PowerPoint. Taylor and Halbritter's performance, occurring jointly with an installation of student multimedia work curated by Anne Wysocki, included fragments of film clips, narration, documentary video, live music, and audience participation. Such work demonstrates the potential value of rethinking our traditional approaches to text by importing methods from other areas.

Verse 2: Parking Lot Experiments and Boombox Experiments

In Oklahoma City throughout 1996, the (then) relatively obscure art/alt-rock band The Flaming Lips staged a series of music installations designed to challenge some of the traditional boundaries of music performance.[2] Coming off a series of accidents, illnesses, a band roster change, and several years of extensive touring, Wayne Coyne, Steven Drozd, and Michael Ivins produced sets of cassettes to be used in what became known as "The Parking Lot Experiments." In the experiments, Coyne gathered groups of fans—and their cars—and at various city parking lots and garages.

At the start of the event, numbered cassettes were distributed to each vehicle. Although each of the 30 cassettes was designed for simultaneous playback, the audio on each varied, sometimes wildly. At the events, audience members (now protomusicians) ran through some practice runs. After debugging reversed tapes, sound levels, and other aspects, Wayne Coyne gave a signal and everyone pressed play.[3]

> Soon sounds appear at one end of the garage, then slowly, it jumps around and the cacophony begins. Moaning, weird instruments, found sound, guitar, drums and bass all contribute. One tape may be nothing more than a drum beat, another, a woman reaching orgasm. Still another may have a few instruments and plenty of fuzz. Every tape is unique, but made in relation to the others. As you wander around, from one end of the cars to the other, stopping to cock yer ear to hear this sound or that, you realize that there is a song, a *composition*, eminating from the cars. Basically, you are hearing 60 + channels of music coming through well over 100 speakers. It is rather overwhelming at times, your pulse rate goes up, folks chatter and the song builds to crescendo. Everyone cheers at the end. (Janecek, n.d./2004)

As Coyne later observed in the liner notes to *Zaireeka*, the events were "a kind of mutated symphony where the musicians were just tape decks" (The Flaming Lips, 1997). Expanding the notion of musical performance to include playing prerecorded music is not especially new. As another participant in the Parking Lot Experiments points out, The Flaming Lips work here parallels in some ways sampling in rap music:

It all sounded way more intense than I could describe. Wayne spent days talking about how crappy it was gonna sound, but for the 23 minutes or so that it lasted, it generally blew me away. It didn't sound anything like a bunch of cars with cruddy tape decks playing weird shit. There was a method to the madness. Sounds weaved in and out and met each other in a way that reminded me of early Public Enemy records, if Aphex Twin and Kevin Shields were part of the Bomb Squad. (Johnson, n.d./2004)

The Flaming Lips continued this type of experimentation with a similar event, this time staged indoors using boomboxes. Again various semi-synchronized tapes and portable players would be distributed to audience members, and, on cue, the band members would direct, orchestra-like, different sections of the audience/orchestra to raise and lower the volumes of their boomboxes (see Fig 6.4).

Following this, The Flaming Lips moved toward producing a mass market version of this work: *Zaireeka*. To play *Zaireeka*, listeners were instructed to assemble four CD players along with three friends. The CD players were to be distributed around the apartment or house and a different disc from the four-CD set placed into each player. As with the Parking Lot Experiments and the Boombox Experiments, some initial coordination is followed by a short countdown and the music sources are all started simultaneously. Listeners moved around the house or apartment as the four tracks mixed together, and the volume of the audio shifted depending on where the listener currently was. Explaining the title of the CD, Coyne acknowledged the simultaneous breakdown/recombination characteristic of symbolic-analytic work, describing the project in the Zaireeka liner notes as,

retarded, but none the less invigorated . . . so anyway it's Zaire fused with Eureka—Zaireeka!! Both of these spheres of thought happening at exactly the same time—a kind of process of decline—simultaneously—but instead of cancelling out the other—one uses the other. Anarchy using inspiration to guide it. And inspiration using anarchy's abandon and power to crash through any road blocks . . . whatever that means??. . . . But somewhere in there is the spark that, I think, holds this concept and these songs together.

Listening to *Zaireeka* is thus a collaborative, contingent, and spatial experience, rather than simply a received artifact.

Fig. 6.4. The Flaming Lips' Boombox Experiment (collage from archival images at < http://www.flaminglips.com/ >)

With each experiment I was more encouraged—and even though it had its limitations, I was discovering the possibilities of using separate sound sources to expand on the ideas of **composing** and **listening**. And at the same time I was finding that the audience liked the idea of participating in their own entertainment . . . it was from this process, these failures and successes, that this four CD concept came into being.

The idea that scratching, sampling, mixing, and extending music spatially are creative has been acknowledged (if still somewhat contested by cultural conservatives) for quite some time by composers such as Philip Glass, Henry Brant, and Steve Reich. Reich's work, "It's Gonna' Rain," for example, builds on brief fragments of street preacher Brother Walter, looped, played over itself, and then shifting out of phase:

I discovered the phasing process by accident. I had two identical loops of Brother Walter saying "It's gonna rain," and I was playing with two inexpensive tape recorders—one jack of my stereo headphones plugged in to machine A, the other into machine B. I had intended to make a specific relations: "It's gonna" on one loop against "rain" on the other. Instead, the two machines happened to be lined up in unison and one of them gradually started to get ahead of the other. The sensation I had in my head was that the sound moved over to my left ear, down to my left shoulder, down my left arm, down my leg, out across the floor to the left, and finally began to reverberate and shake and become the sound I was looking for—"it's gonna/It's gonna rain/rain"—and then it started going the other way and came back together in the center of my head. When I heard that, I realized it was more interesting than any one particular relationship, because it was the process (of gradually passing through all of the canonic relationships) making an entire piece, and not just a moment in time. (S. Reich, 2002, pp. 20–21)

Although our culture has come to accept this experimentation in some forms of music, we are less comfortable with the idea that routine types of communication, such as writing, can be validly composed from nonoriginal fragments.

INTERFACE AS DECONSTRUCTIVE ARCHITECTURE: ARTICULATING HETEROGENEOUS SPACES

Architecture does not precede philosophy. Space is produced as such by the particular discourse maintained by philosophy, and there is no philosophy without space. Architecture and philosophy are effects of the same transaction, effects that can never be separated.
—Wigley (1995, p. 22)

The very heterogeneity of the definition of architecture—space, action, and movement—makes it into that event, that place of shock, or that place of the invention of ourselves. The event is the place where the rethinking and reformulation of the different elements of architecture, many of which have resulted in or added to contemporary social inequities, may lead to their solution.
—Tschumi (1996, p. 258)

Communication has long been articulated as both a process and an artifact. We communicate with each other, we read communications, and we build communication networks. We can communicate about communication within communications. Although the term *communication* seems to do a wonderful job of capturing both object and action, we continue to treat those artifacts—the objects of communication—as relatively inert and external objects. In other words, we have succeeded in articulating the term *communication* as *either* an action or an object, but we have done less at thinking about how to fully support communication as simultaneously object and action. For example, we pay a great deal of attention to interfaces for communication software, analyzing usability, customizing features, and asking for revisions to various aspects. All of these are important things to pay attention to. Yet for the most part, the communications that we craft are somewhat like dead ends: They do not support communication, they merely trigger it or record it.[4] In this chapter, I discuss information spaces that communicate doubly: they both support and are composed of communication.[5] Current information architecture is a useful, but limited starting point because a useful articulation of interface for symbolic-analytic work has to go beyond utility, much as architecture needed to look beyond utility for its own value. This is, in fact, Hegel's definition of architecture: anything in a building that "did not point to utility" (Tschumi, 1996, p. 32).

In a surprising way here, then, architecture here becomes the Derridean "supplement"—the meaning outside of the text. This is what I want to talk about: writing or textuality as deconstructivist architecture.

Information Architecture as Support for Traditional Work

Information architecture suggests a starting point for our exploration of the possibilities of new information spaces for work. Information architects have succeeded in constructing a workable articulation of interfaces that support symbolic inhabitation. Users of information, from the information architecture perspective, work within interfaces, navigating them to locate needed information. Like many traditional architects, information architects bring order to space, allowing people to move in reasoned and self-determined ways.

As information architect Chiou (2003) commented,

> When I'm asked, "How did you become an information architect?" my immediate answer is, "I was already halfway there by being an architect." Although I say this partly in jest, it certainly has some truth to it. Information architecture has a great deal to do with traditional architecture—especially in the ability of each discipline to plan and connect various important elements together. (n.p.)

For Chiou, architecture relies on a careful balance of form and function, with emphasis placed primarily on function and purpose. Chiou and others in information architecture draw useful concepts from traditional architecture (such as design languages, collaboration, and planning), attempting to construct rational, usable, and clear spaces that further specific types of purposes and use. Of paramount importance is the modernist maxim "form follows function," particularly in the battle to bring order to masses of confusing information.

As Wurman (p. 15) set the scene in his foundational edited collection, *Information Architects,*

> There is a tsunami of data that is crashing into the beaches of the civilized world. This is a tidal wave of unrelated, growing data in bits and bytes, coming in an unorganized, uncontrolled, incoherent cacophony of foam. It's filled with flotsam and jetsam. It's filled with sticks and bones and shells of inanimate and animate life. None of it is easily related, none of it comes with any organizational methodology.

As it washes up on our beaches, we see people in suits and ties skipping along the shoreline, men and women in fine shirts and blouses dressed for business. We see graphic designers and government officials, all getting their shoes wet and slowly submerging in the dense trough of stuff. Their trousers and slacks soaked, they walk stupidly into the water, smiling—a false smile of confidence and control. The tsunami is a wall of data—data produced at greater and greater speed, greater and greater amounts to store in memory, amounts that double, it seems, with each sunset. On tape, on paper, sent by streams of light. Faster, more and more and more. (p. 15)[6]

We have to wonder, why do we articulate data as something that will kill us, besoil us? If it were the sheer amount, we might as readily rail about blades of grass, paperclips, or office chairs, but we do not. The reason we tend to think of information as something that contaminates us is our need to *manage* information, to control it.

For example, Rosenfeld and Moreville's (2002) widely used *Information Architecture* (a text I use in my own information architecture courses) describes "the main job of an information architect" as someone who

- Clarifies the *mission* and the *vision* for the site, balancing the needs of its sponsoring organization and the needs of its audiences.
- Determines what *content* and *functionality* the site will contain.
- Specifies how users will find information in the site by defining its *organization, navigation, labeling,* and *searching systems.*
- Maps out how the site will accommodate *change* and *growth* over time. (p. 11)

For many (perhaps most) information spaces, these are extremely important activities in a society overwhelmed by information. Certainly controlling information in certain circumstances will continue to be valuable and necessary. Yet information architecture, articulated as the interface equivalent of contemporary modernist architecture, is not capable of providing an environment proper for the articulatory, symbolic-analytic work emerging in the datacloud.

Focus on Creating Clarity

Information architecture tends to assume a functional divide between environments of development and environments of use, paralleling the divide between the two activities in interface design in general as discussed in the previous chapter. The information architect is based on a combination of scientific reasoning and collective experience to design authoritative spaces. Current information spaces are developed using powerful and complex interfaces (Visio, Dreamweaver, etc.), but the resulting spaces typically offer much less power and complexity.

Usability testing, a common practice in information architecture, appears to offer the opportunity for users to exert influence on the design of these spaces. Yet as currently practiced, usability acts as a method for verifying assumptions about relatively bounded functions: *Can you locate the page listing open hours for the library? What information do you think you'll see if you click this button labeled, "Staff"? Did you find the information you were looking for?*

There are other forms of usability inquiry that allow much broader influence from users of an interface, such as contextual inquiry and participatory design. Contextual inquiry involves researchers observing users in their natural habitat (office, classroom, etc.), gathering information on the concrete environments in which an interface will be used to compensate for external factors (workflow, space, etc.). Participatory design goes one step further and involves the users explicitly in design discussions. (The field emerged from work in workplace automation as an attempt to give workers a voice in their own working conditions.) In addition, usability tends to construct users as victims, as Spinuzzi (2003) argued, who need to be rescued by the designer who will bring order to the user's world.

In general, information architecture tends to focus on usability inquiry that addresses relatively low-level, functional issues. The interfaces that are developed tend to focus on simplicity and neutrality. Useful interfaces for symbolic-analytic work, however, require a more complex and open interface.

Overriding Focus on Information Access and Retrieval

The quest for simplicity in information architecture grows out of the assumption that, in the majority of cases, users want to locate a specific piece of information. There is no denying the fact that information access and retrieval are crucial functions of working with a complex body of information: If a user cannot locate information, he or she cannot do anything with it.

Yet as with the related issue of clarity, locating information is only one small portion of what is required of an interface that adequately supports advanced symbolic-analytic work. Information architecture has little to say about complex practices such as rearranging information fragments, tracking various possibilities over time, and storing alternatives for later use. When information architecture does take up such topics, it does so in relatively unproblematized ways, such as how to make a search interface clearer or how to store purchases in a shopping cart form until checkout. Yet symbolic-analytic work requires a primary focus on such issues.

Assumption of Order and Certainty

Perhaps most important, information architecture works under the assumption that order—certainty—can and should be brought to chaotic information. In general, in this system, navigation systems should be clear, labels should be unambiguous, and superfluous elements should be removed wherever possible. If an interface object does not have a discernable, useful function, it should be removed.

Symbolic-analytic work, however, requires a certain—sometimes a very large—amount of contingency within an interface. Often, apparently irrelevant and unrelated objects gain meaning when they are juxtaposed with other objects. Symbolic-analytic work is an ongoing oscillation between chaos and order, with neither term necessarily superior to the other. For many projects, if a situation can be articulated in simple, easy terms, it is not really a situation worth dealing with.

Although information architecture provides an important starting point for considering spaces that support symbolic-analytic work, it is only a starting point, not a goal. The design of clean, clear, efficient interfaces tends to short-circuit important contingencies necessary to symbolic-analytic work. In a sense, one might think of information architecture as modeled on a traditional, modernist form of architecture and symbolic-analytic work modeled on a deconstructivist architecture—a form of architecture that learns from modernist architecture, but moves beyond it to deal with issues of contingency, complexity, and lack of clarity as potentially positive rather than negative aspects.

Deconstructivist Architecture

I do not want to negate the importance of those functionalist approaches to designing textual spaces. Information architecture will continue to grow in importance as increasing amounts of our lives are spent online. Yet I want to add to those beginnings with a brief sketch of the sorts of concerns that deconstructive architecture brings to the project of building spaces.

Deconstructivist architecture, like communication, is both an action and an object. The spaces created in deconstructivist architecture retain symbolic force, but do not degenerate into pure (presumably neutral) function or simple, universal meanings. The work of deconstructivist architecture parallels and can inform work on articulation theory by bridging ideological and material realms; it can contribute to symbolic-analytic work by acknowledging and working within information as contingent and mutually constructing space.

In deconstructivist architecture, as theorists and practitioners such as Rem Koolhaas and Bernard Tschumi articulate it, architecture is both space and action—but the actions are not necessarily determined automatically by the space or relate primarily to the space as a form of building (or textual) worship.

Our primary object of study here—the interface—constitutes a textual site for deconstruction, both architectural and philosophical. Texts of various types have long functioned at the crossroads of philosophy and architecture. As Wigley (1995) demonstrated in *The Architecture of Deconstruction: Derrida's Haunt*, philosophy has commonly, if uneasily, articulated its work as a form of architecture: Kant

> employs architecture to describe metaphysics in the *Critique of Pure Reason* (although Kant hastens to subordinate the profession of architecture itself to a decorative art in *The Critique of Judgement*). (p. 13)

Architecture functions as a central concept for Heidegger, who equates building with thinking (Wigley, 1995). As Tschumi (1996) argued,

> [D]econstructing architecture involved dismantling its conventions, using concepts derived both from architecture and from elsewhere— from cinema, literary criticism, and other disciplines. For if the limits between different domains of thought have gradually vanished in the past twenty years, the same phenomenon applies to architecture, which now entertains relations with cinema, philosophy, and psychoanalysis (to cite only a few examples) in an intertextuality subversive of modernist autonomy. (p. 199)

Architecture has a long history as a general textual practice as well. The distinction between architecture and construction—architect versus building contractor—articulates architecture as a symbolic activity tenden-tially located outside of function, but always colonizing it. Similarly, texts, when they succeed, have material effects. Political slogans inspire political actions in the real world, and architectural sketches and plans direct the construction of buildings. As the function of textuality has shifted during the last half century or so, with the rise of heavily mediated societies and the spread of the information economy (and, one could add, the informa-tion society), our relations to texts have shifted. As texts have come, in symbolic-analytic work and articulation theory (among others), to involve the manipulation of fragments of information, architecture, as Tschumi (1995) articulated it,

> attempts to play with the fragments of a given reality at the same time
> as the rational structure or abstract concepts, while constantly ques-
> tioning the nature of architectural signs. These fragments of reality . . .
> unavoidably introduce ideological and cultural concerns. (p. 8)

Tschumi's work—and that of other deconstructivist architects—Is valuable to the project of articulating spaces for symbolic-analytic work in the datacloud. Deconstructive architecture succeeds on two key levels: material and symbolic. Although battles rage over the appropriateness and aesthetic appearance of much of the contemporary architecture, the fact remains that these architects have taken up core principles of deconstruc-tion and postmodernism and *made them work*.

Tschumi (1996) provided a set of maxims for understanding decon-structive architecture *Architecture and Disjunction*. Tschumi attempted to frame a response to Vince Scully's dismissal of deconstructivist architec-ture as "a moment of supreme silliness that deconstructs and self-destruc-ts" (cited in Tschumi, 1996, p. 228).

Table 6.1 condenses, in an overly simplistic way, Tschumi's six con-cepts for deconstructivist architecture, with definitions and examples drawn from a variety of sources.[7] The six concepts are not a coherent framework for rethinking architecture; they are more along the lines of "six important ways of resisting in architecture." Tschumi's overall goals, con-sistent with deconstructivist architecture, involve creating spaces that are inhabited, not merely decorative. Deconstructivist architecture both sup-ports and challenges people, providing them spaces to move within while commenting on conditions of contemporary life. At the same time, decon-structivist architects, at least in Tschumi's articulation of the practice, are not all-knowing, godlike figures who stand above, dictating use. Rather,

Table 6.1. Tschumi's (1996) Six Concepts for Deconstructive Architecture

Defamiliarization	Makes the Visible the Familiar
Mediated Metropolitan Shock	overcome information overload/numbing
Destructuring	Deconstruction
Superimposition	layering representation (across event, subject, etc.)
Cross-programming	Juxtaposition of different activities in same space
Event	putting people in action in spaces

people interact with those spaces, changing their meanings in ways that the architect cannot foresee.

Whereas traditional architecture (and information architecture) would deem contingency and chaos as negative aspects, deconstructive architecture recognizes the productive and creative potential in those characteristics. Just as important, deconstructive architecture frequently involves social commentary in ways commensurate with the social project of articulation theory. So we might consider the work of deconstructive architecture as something akin to Stuart Hall's understanding of the place of postmodernism in relation to articulation theory—not a rejection, but a recuperation and reclaiming of terrain and power. The fragmenting impulses contained (and exploded) by these gestures do not obliterate opportunities for meaning; they make new meanings possible.

Toward Interface

This detour through music and architecture suggests some key concerns and strategies for interfaces that support symbolic-analytic work. First, the emphasis on breaking down artifacts—from songs to buildings to texts—is an important work habit in the information age. Breakdown opens up possibilities for recombination. Second, symbolic-analytic workers require support for maintaining and organizing large volumes of data (and facilities for moving data around). Third, texts are participatory and contingent, rather than passively received: Even the act of pressing play should be considered performance. Buildings are performances enacted by their occupants, who articulate differing forms of meaning by their presence. To ignore those contributions is to lose sight of the function of architecture. Fourth, choices about information—how its combined, filtered, and arranged—have moral consequences; the symbolic-analytic worker should not strive to be neutral and invisible because that stance ignores that artifacts have politics, to use Langdon Winner's phrase. Users should, occasionally at least, be pushed to consider their relations to the technology, to the culture around them.

Notes

1. In the quoted sequence here, from the documentary *Scratch*, DJ's Steinski and Jazzy Jay are shot in separate interviews and then cut and remixed later to provide an interweaved running commentary. This editing practice, a common one in film, highlights and parallels similar practices in turntablism.

2. Material in this section is a compilation of several key Web sites documenting the experiments: < http://www.janecek.com/parkinglot.html > and < http://www.wbr.com/flaminglips/cmp/parking.htm > .

3. The punctuation and spelling are left as in the original informal Web page report on the event.

4. That is not to say that traditional communication is not interactive—it clearly is. My point here is that our current technologies could do a better job of supporting that interaction and contingency.

5. One might argue here that software invariably communicates by suggesting to users different ways of structuring their working and thinking. That is exactly my point.

6. To which I thought, *Cool! More! More information!*

7. I have developed a slightly more detailed series of parallels between composition and deconstructive architecture in "Composition as Architecture."

7

SOME REARTICULATIONS: EMERGENT SYMBOLIC-ANALYTIC SPACES

When software design teams maintain conventional assumptions—emphasizing design as a logic for making the separate entities of practice and tools equivalent—it may appear that design is neutral in regard to competing interests in users' workplaces. However, when designers regard . . . work as a process of tools and practices that co-produce each other, it is much harder to ignore the political side of design. From this vantage point, even benign, logical design choices such as data formats or methods to access data take on a dimension of power in user's workplaces.
—Mirel (2003, p. 305)

In this chapter, I identify some interfaces that provide some level of support for typical symbolic-analytic activities such as filtering and arranging. These programs are still relatively rare, but they provide glimpses of emerging possibilities and suggestions about tendencies we should examine and encourage.

One relatively visible area of support is appearing in the development and use of Weblogs. Weblogs are an online genre that have gained popularity during the early 21st century. They were initiated in the early 1990s as a method for commenting on, responding to, and pointing toward Web sites. Although there is quite a bit of variation in the genre, weblogs in general follow a journal format in which news items (links, announcements, gems found out on the Web, etc.) are posted to the top of the main page, pushing older items down (see Fig. 7.1).

Weblogs provide an excellent example of active production. Although early Weblogs served as relatively simple diaries of Web reading that were

Fig. 7.1. BoingBoing Weblog < http://www.boingboing.net/ >

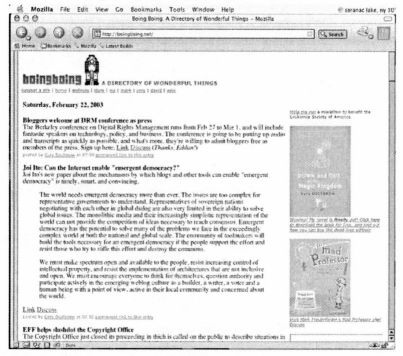

updated manually (via cut and paste) in HTML (and, as such, still separat-ed consumption and production), newer tools are beginning to provide sup-port for more complex information-manipulation activities.

For example, the Weblog browser NetNewsWire (NNW) originated as a simple, but extremely useful, information management tool: NNW allows users to monitor updates to news sources on the Web in a relatively com-pact and fast manner. Users "subscribe" to RSS feeds—specially designed Web pages that contain compacted information about ongoing updates to a main site.

NNW monitors these RSS feeds from other Weblogs to produce an up-to-date index of large volumes of Weblogs (my own set of feeds frequently exceeds 200 weblogs). Whereas traditional Weblog readers view Weblogs through a standard Web browser interface, NNW transforms the RSS streams into a highly condensed, dynamic information display (see Fig. 7.2).

Fig. 7.2. NetNewsWire RSS feed browser.

The index in this figure provides a list of Weblogs being monitored (on the left), titles of currents stories on the Weblog (top right), and stories themselves (bottom right). Users who want to view the full Web page can double click the entry in the headlines to launch a standard Web browser if the user wants to see the story in its native format.

NNW and other RSS browsers gained wide usage among not only Weblog browsers in general, but also in that group of browsers who were also producers: weblog authors who used the tool to monitor news streams to develop content for their own Weblogs. NNW developers then began adding facilities for not only browsing streams, but also taking notes (via a simple notepad) and posting to Weblogs of various types (see Fig 7.3). (Weblogs commonly have open standards, allowing programs from one company to produce texts that are readable in a Weblog in its native format.)

Similarly, Tinderbox (Bernstein, 2003), a more general information work environment developed by Eastgate (producers of venerable hypertext-authoring program Storyspace) provides an information working space that

**Fig. 7.3. NetNewsWire posting information gathered from one Weblog
to another.**

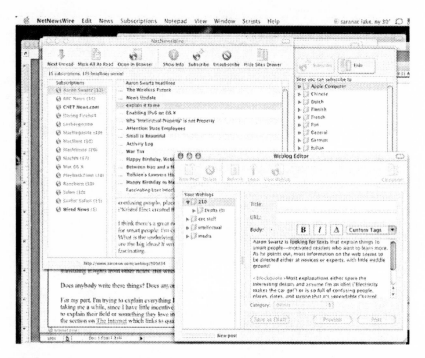

directly supports advanced symbolic-analytic work by organizing itself
around chunks of information that can be moved around, nested, transformed, filtered, and exported (see Fig 7.4). The nexus of advanced information work and Weblogs is reaffirmed in Tinderbox via support for producing Weblogs from Tinderbox files.

Somewhat denser development environments can be found in media
production tools such as Macromedia Flash and Dreamweaver, Final Cut
Pro, or ProTools, discussed earlier. These spaces excel at providing methods for importing information, filtering and modifying it, and collaborating.
Other more specialized environments such as Macromedia's Central for
Internet application development offer even more robust support for some
forms of symbolic-analytic work. Central was designed to address a set of
needs consistent with symbolic-analytic work, including interapplication
cooperation, data transportability via XML, understanding context, and
encouraging collaboration with other developers (Lynch, 2004).

Fig. 7.4. Information work in Tinderbox.

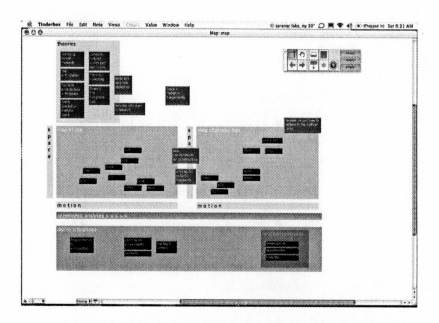

One striking difference between traditional interfaces and the symbolic-analytic interfaces offered by applications like Microsoft Word is the focus of these applications on information movement and information arrangement. Whereas applications like Word or WordPerfect represent a relatively isolated space, into which information enters only grudgingly, the interface of NetNewsWire prioritizes movement. Furthermore, information is represented at differing levels of abstraction to support skimming as well as deep reading and writing: headline, summary, and link to full article on the Web.

Such tools represent an important step toward realizing forms of communication that do not prioritize either consumption or production. By seeing information not as something simply to be consumed, but to be manipulated, moved around, reconnected, and redistributed, programs such as NetNewsWire and Tinderbox suggest new forms of communication and work: not simply about the production of original ideas, but the construction of shared spaces; not simply about producing or consuming information, but working and living within it; not simply about universal truths and meanings, but about the confluence of local and global contexts, resistance, and change.

Work within these spaces also resembles other disruptive and productive activities ranging from deconstructive (information) architecture to turntablism. Weblog authors search for bits of information, juxtapose pieces, and comment on them. Webloggers are geek DJs.

One might rightfully ask, at this point, where are we left after this long discourse, through histories of interface development, critiques of software, discussions of architecture, and more? In my attempt to outline a space for developing an understanding of how to work productively (rather than resistantly) within the datacloud, I attempt to outline a repertoire of strategies.

First, we must learn to understand learning and work in new ways: Creativity is no longer the production of original texts, but the ability to gather, filter, rearrange, and construct new texts—symbolic-analytic work, articulations.

Second, as interfaces have shifted from an emphasis on depth to surface, users have begun to work with information in new ways. Although interfaces will never be able to hold all of the information that symbolic-analysts need at any point that should not be their goal. Users need to have available to them as much information as possible and robust methods for moving information around, virtually and physically. Users seem to be learning new methods for reading interfaces containing more information than the previous generation knew how to deal with.

Third, information is always associated with political and cultural meanings. This is not to say that pieces of information come to us with instructions on how to position and use them, but that they do possess tendential forces suggesting ways to articulate them. Moreover, even when we contest those meanings, our own use of those pieces is bound up in political and social acts.

Fourth, those surfaces must be translated into working spaces if we are to begin working along the lines suggested by symbolic-analytic work. Current software tends to construct text construction as a romanticist creation that springs forth from the brow of the writer. Symbolic-analytic work, however, involves the movement, filtering, and connection of existing chunks of information. Such work demands a more spatial environment than currently supported.

Fifth, and finally, these new spaces cannot be founded simply on a traditional approach to information architecture. The requirements for contingency, information overload, and ongoing re- and deconstruction require new types of architecture more attuned to contemporary life.

8

CODA: A TEXT IN FRAGMENTS

I begin, in postmodern style, with a pastiche of quotations from, at first sign, somewhat disparate sources. . . .
—David Morley (1996, p. 326)

While at AT&T Labs, four colleagues and I had the opportunity to study a very large sample of monitored—IM interactions—over 21,000 IM conversations involving 437 users conducted from mid-2000 to late 2001. . . .

Our study suggests that some people seem to be very effective at discussing complex work topics using nothing more than text. And since all users often multitask while engaged in IM conversations, it would be a mistake to tightly integrate IM with certain applications, thereby making it difficult for users to jump from one application to another.

Our results also suggest that the characteristics of heavy IM   use—multiple, brief, intermittent interactions throughout the day whereby the lines of communication are more or less left open for spontaneous conversation—mirror the nature of impromptu pair-wise interactions in other media. This finding suggests that other tools intended to supplement or work with IM should seek to support the characteristics of the sort of lightweight, unplanned interactions we witness each day in the places we work.
—Isaacs (2003, n.p.)

The following examples highlight the breadth of the digital divide today:

- Those with a college degree are more than *eight* times as likely to have a computer at home and nearly *sixteen* times as likely to have home Internet access, as those with an elementary school education.
- A high-income household in an urban area is more than *twenty times* as likely as a rural, low-income household to have Internet access.

- A child in a low-income White family is *three times* as likely to have Internet access as a child in a comparable African American family and *four times* as likely to have access as children in a comparable Hispanic household.
- A wealthy household of Asian/Pacific Islander descent is nearly *thirteen times* as likely to own a computer as a poor African American household, and nearly *thirty-four times* as likely to have Internet access.
- Finally, a child in a dual-parent White household is nearly *twice* as likely to have Internet access as a child in a White single-parent household, while a child in a dual-parent African American family is almost *four times* as likely to have access as a child in a single-parent Black household.

The data reveal that the digital divide—the disparities in access to telephones, personal computers (PCs), and the Internet across certain demographic groups—still exists and, in many cases, has widened significantly. The gap for computers and Internet access has generally grown larger by categories of education, income, and race

—National Telecommunications and Information Administration Report (n/d 2004)

—Rodriguez (2003)

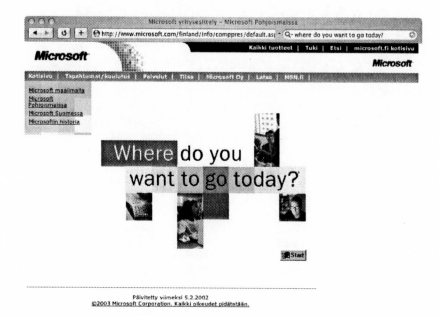

—Microsoft Finland, < http://www.microsoft.com/ finland/info/com/ finland/info/compress/default.asp >

The situation looks and sometimes feels desperate, but we have to learn to live inside it (there is no going back). In the Post, within a world of fragments, small locations, microchips, salvation has always been miniaturized, cut down to size. We can begin to draw small lessons from unsuspected sources.
—Hebdige, (1989, p. 232)

I'm speaking slowly to get it right. It's my book after all, so I'm responsible for getting it right. The loneliness of voices stored on tape. By the time you listen to this, I'll no longer remember what I said. I'll be an old message by then, buried under many new messages. The machine makes everything a message, which narrows the range of discourse and destroys the poetry of nobody home. Home is a failed idea. People are no longer home or not home. They're either picking up or not picking up. . . .

The machine cut him off.
—DeLillo, (1991, pp. 92-93)

By 5.50 it was really light outside. We had lost our lead ship, but Lieutenant Godfrey, our navigator, informs me that we had arranged for that contingency. We have an assembly point in the sky above the little island of Yakushima, southeast of Kyushu at 9.10. We are to circle there and wait for the rest of the formation.

Our genial bombardier, Lieutenant Levy, comes over to invite me to take his front-row seat in the transparent nose of the ship, and I accept eagerly. From that vantage point in space, seventeen thousand feet above the Pacific, one gets a view of hundreds of miles on all sides, horizontally and vertically. At that height the vast ocean below and the sky above seem to merge into one great sphere.

I was on the inside of that firmament, riding above the giant mountains of white cumulus clouds, letting myself be suspended in infinite space. One hears the whirl of motors behind one, but it soon becomes insignificant against the immensity all around and is before long swallowed by it. There comes a point where space also swallows time and one lives through eternal moments filled with an oppressive loneliness, as though all life had suddenly vanished from the earth and you are the only one left, a lone survivor travelling endlessly through interplanetary space.

My mind soon returns to the mission I am on. Somewhere beyond these vast mountains of white clouds ahead of me there lies Japan, the land of our enemy. . . . Captain Bock informs me that we are about to start our climb to bombing altitude. . . . We shall soon meet our lead ship and proceed to the final stage of our journey. We reached Yakushima at 9.12 and there about four thousand feet ahead of us, was *The Great Artiste* with its precious load. . . . I saw Lieutenant Godfrey and Sergeant Curry strap on their parachutes and decided to do likewise... We started circling. . . . We kept on circling. . . . It was 12.01 and the goal of our mission had arrived.

We heard the pre-arranged signal on our radio, put on our arc welder's glasses and watched tensely the manoeuvrings of the strike ship about a half a mile in front of us.

"There she goes!" someone said.

Out of the belly of *The Great Artiste* what looked like a black object went downward.

—William Lawrence, "Atomic Bombing of Nagasaki Told by Flight Member," NYT 9 September 1945 (cited in Hebdige, 1989, p. 228)

When the geek bestows his highest accolade on some software—that it's *cool*—he is making an aesthetic judgment. It is cool because it is original and beautiful; it has crossed a conventional boundary, and solved a problem in a surprising way. Cool software is, perhaps, elegantly simple, or it can perform an operation that no one had previously thought of, or it is lovely in the sense that only one steeped in software design could fully appreciate. It reflects insight and dexterity on the part of its designer. The pleasure in devising or beholding it has nothing to do with its likely market value, and everything to do with its artistry—its cleverness, its acuity, its perfection. It is the same pleasure the artist (or an art critic) takes in a painting that is both original and powerful, or the musician takes in a musical composition (or in her performance) that takes the medium to a new level of intensity, grace, and mastery. It is an *insider's* appreciation. "Cool" was, after all, the term used by jazz musicians of the bee-bop generation who broke through the melodious conventions of the age and introduced a new aesthetic—a new rhythm and sound.

—R. Reich (2001, p. 54)

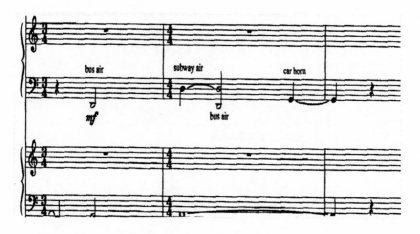

—Detail from S. Reich, "City Life," lines for tape samples of bus, subway, and car horns

Today, the two areas of investigation most likely to provide fertile discoveries are located in our disjoined terms: spaces (through new technology and structures, or—to use the title of a conference at Columbia University—through 'glue and microchips') and events (through new programmatic, functional, or social relations, through the spectacle of everyday life). One argument for the interchangeability of the two terms can be found in the new media technology that at once defines and activates space, such as electronic façades that are both enclosure and spectacle.

—Bernard Tschumi, (1996, pp. 22-23)

You are children, playing a game, but nonetheless a master of eloquence. Your success at the game depends on your persuasive ardor as much as your ability. Positions and figures in space are the power of rhetoric.

The same holds true for the novice or the expert. Such is the teaching of Menander of Laodicea, known as Rhetor, in his exhortations in praise of cities.

—Koolhaas et al. (2001, p. 23)

To better understand the rhetorical and technological competencies involved in data reporting, researchers need to investigate the ways in which various features and functions of database applications enhance or constrain rhetorical choices, including the effects of advances in program capabilities and interfaces on reporting.

—Mirel (1996, p. 109)

This is the story. These are all the various things that have happened to me in the last few weeks. But now, as I flick through the book, I see only the mess I have made. Words, sentences, paragraphs, whole pages, scoured with black marks. Mistakes. The noise gets in everywhere. Pages are ripped, or torn out completely; some discarded, others taped into new positions. There are smudges of dirt, of food, of blood. The marks where once a pressed flower lay; stains of clorophyll, pollen, the tiny fragments of a petal.

—Jeff Noon (p. 11)

—Pressed flower found in the pages of a copy of *The Happy Isles of Oceania* (Theroux), Purchased at the Birchbark Bookstore, Parishville, NY

—The Sims (collage from screenshots at official Web site)

Your parents were like, "Don't touch the turntable! Don't touch the record! You're gonna' ruin it!"
—Cut Chemist, Scratch (Qtd. in Blondheim, Meza, & Pray, 2001)

Fragments of architecture (bits of walls, of rooms, of streets, of ideas) are all one actually sees. These fragments are like beginnings without ends. There is always a split between fragments that are real and fragments that are virtual, between memory and fantasy. These splits have no existence other than being the passage from one fragment to another. They are relays rather than signs. They are traces. They are in-between.

It is not the clash between these contradictory fragments that counts, but the movement between them. And this invisible movement is neither a part of language nor of structure (language or structure are words specific to a mode of reading architecture that does not fully apply in the context of pleasure); it is nothing but a constant and mobile relationship inside language itself.
—Tschumi, (1996, p. 95)

Jon had an incredible amount of music, with what we call a left-foot approach to it. He was into African and weird New York productions, everything up to [minimalist composer] Steve Reich.
—Matt Black, Coldcut (Cited in Reighley, 2000, p. 81)

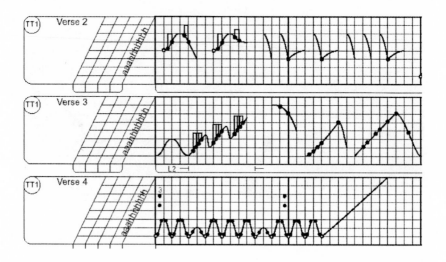

—Detail from Turntablist Transcription Method, *Battlesounds*
< http://www.battlesounds.com/transcription.html >

I still do charity shops and boot sales. I had a wicked find the other day,
some very obscure electronic records. A collection of weird electronics
from Czechoslovakia, John Cage's *Fontana Mix* in mint condition, John
Cage's *Prepared Pianos*, never been played. All for three quid each!
—Jonathon More, Cold Cut, (cited in Reighley, 2000, p. 83)

In this battle for precedence, one term commands originary status by
casting the opposing term as inessential—by becoming the ground
condition from which the other differs as an addition or supplement.
The opposition between architecture's physical presence as a building
and its existence as an abstract institution defines the paradigmatic
axis of this geometry of supplements; the syntagmatic axi is defined as
the two worlds manufacture the sense of necessity that will determine
the order of precedence along the pardigmatic [sic]. In each case, the
character of essentiality being strived for is related to purposefulness.
Architecture's difference from building, and its status as a supplement,
hinges in each case on the lever of use. When building is defined by
function, architecture is seen as an addition or superlative marked by
its lack: Utility is the dominant term. Further, utility is seen as ground
condition for determining meaning—including that which art, as a purposeful activity, claims to offer. If a supplement is the sign of the presence of grafted texts/arguments, then in this case the text of art is grafted onto the body of the building as architecture.

But the idea of supplement is also understood as that-which-makes-up-for-deficiencies: " . . . supplementation is possible only because of an originary lack." Architecture would not be continuously re-invented if it weren't felt that building itself was somehow incomplete. This ordinary lack is not *in* or *of* the building, however. It is rather the building's necessary (objective) distance/difference from the subject—a distance that can only be overcome by the supplement of analogy, or reading (which, of course, still leaves the actual Other ever derived, deferred). The projected selfness that constitutes reading masks the object as it frames it into a particular reading set. The supplementary concept of architecture becomes the means by which understand the idea building itself; it becomes the reading of building. This occurs not only through a dialectical understanding of building as a pre-architectural or non-architectural condition, but also through architecture's structuring presence as the frame or context which isolates for us the territory of building. Those central issues like structure of function, "which appears to explain everything"—by which we label the concept of architecture as an inessential superlative or enhanced "supplementary" condition— are themselves ineluctably caught up in the contextual net that determines their own reading. Their centrality is not given or immediate: it is finally not of the building itself, but of the architectural experience of the building.

—Pfau and Jones, (1987, pp. 46-48)

In making the four-channel video work *Dachau 1974*, my experience as a weaver directly influenced the basic structuring of the work. The content itself was taped in 1974 at the former concentration camp, Dachau. The symmetry of the architecture and the *present* ambience of this space were the focus of the recordings. The past was recorded only insofar as the sounds of the voices of the present commingled with the feeling absorbed in the wood and revealed in the structure of forms which no amount of time can erase. In retrospect, form a historical perspective, what seems most unique about Dachau symbolically is the expression of that darker side of the human spirit, manifested here through the use of specific tools and techniques of a highly sophisticated and efficient nature.

Once the material for the work was gathered, I turned to the ancient technology of the loom to help solve problems I'd long been having in working with video.

The technology of the loom and the art of weaving both literally and metaphorically represent the combining of many separate elements (literally in the form of threads) to develop patterns that evolve in time to create fabric. That is, the rhythmic body time (as expressed through hand movements)/eye/mind relationship of the individual weaver works in harmony with the laws of the machine itself. For a particular work, the weaver passes weft threads over and under the warp threads of the loom, which as been threaded (programmed) by the weaver so that preselected pattern possibilities remain for the weaver to develop, or ignore, when creating a work.

—Korot (2002, p. 85)

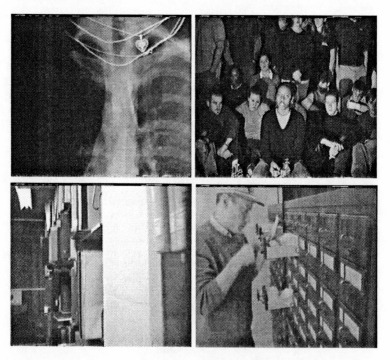

—Four Scenes from Todd Taylor's *New Media Composition Live* [Video adapted from conference presentation]

Tupelo sleeps on the other bed, breathing gently, and sometimes sighing. I have covered the lamp with an old shirt from my bag; now the light barely touches the girl, but falls steadily on the notebook as I write. I have taken advantage of the needle's sweetness, to hold the day in words; and the pages I have just written, and the pages already written, they seem to make a kind of sense now. I have knowledge of the story once more, my own story, my place in the story.

—Noon (2002, p. 215)

REFERENCES

Adams, Nick. (n.d./2004). A history of adventure. *The Colossal Cave Adventure Page.* http://www.rickadams.org/adventure/a_history.html (April 4, 2004).

Althusser, Louis. (1971). Ideology and ideological state apparatuses (notes towards an investigation). In Ben Brewster (Trans.), *Lenin and philosophy and other essays* (pp. 127-186). New York: Monthly Review Press.

Anderson, Laurie. (1982) Walking and falling. [Audio recording.] In *Big science.* Burbank, CA: Warner Bros.

Apple Computer. (2003). *iChat* version 2.0 (v145). Cupertino, CA: Author.

Bernstein, Mark. (2003). *Tinderbox* (Version 2.0). Watertown, MA: Eastgate.

Blondheim, Brad, Ernest Meza (Producers), and Doug Pray (Director). (2001). *Scratch.* New York: Palm Pictures.

Bolter, Jay David, and Richard Grusin. (2000). *Remediation: Understanding new media.* Cambridge, MA: MIT Press.

Brasseur, Lee E. (1994). How computer graphing programs change the graphic design process; Results of research on the fill pattern feature. *Journal of Computer Documentation, 18*(4), 4-20.

Burstein, Laura. (2003, October 20). *Laura Burstein's Moblog* [Web site]. < http://lburstein.textamerica.com. >

Byrne, David. (2003, September). Learning to love PowerPoint. *Wired* 11(09) [Web site]. < http://www.wired.com/wired/archive/11.09/ppt1.html. >

Carluccio, John. (n.d./2004) Turntablist transcription. *Battlesounds* [Web site]. http://www.battlesounds.com/transcription.html.

Carroll, John M. (1990). *The Nurnberg funnel: Designing minimalist instruction for practical computer skill.* Cambridge, MA: MIT Press.

Chaplin, Charles (Producer and Director). (1936). *Modern times* [Motion picture]. Burbank, CA: Warner Bros.

Davis, D. Diane. (1998). (Non)fiction('s) addiction(s): A narcoanalysis of virtual worlds. In Cynthia Haynes & Jan Rune Holmevik (Eds.), *High wired: On the design, use, and theory of educational MOOs* (pp. 267-285). Ann Arbor: University of Michigan Press.

Davis, Joshua. (2003, June). If we run out of batteries, this war is screwed. *Wired* 11(06) [Web site]. < http://www.wired.com/wired/archive/11.06/battlefield_pr.html. >

Deeley, Michael (Producer), and Ridley Scott (Director). (1982). *Blade Runner*. The Ladd Company.

Deeley, Michael, Barry Spikings (Producers), and Nicolas Roeg (Director). (1976). *The man who fell to earth*. London: British Lion Film Corp.

Deleuze, Gilles, and Claire Parnet. (1989). *Dialogues*. Columbia University Press.

Deleuze, Gilles, and Felix Guattari. (1987). *One thousand plateaus: Capitalism and schizophrenia* (Brian Massumi, Trans.) Minneapolis: University of Minnesota Press.

DeLillo, Don. (1991). *Mao II*. New York: Viking.

Digidesign. (2000). ProTools LE v. 5.01. Daly City, CA: Avid Technology.

Dreamweaver 3. (2000). San Francisco, CA: Macromedia.

Dreamweaver MX. (2003). San Francisco, CA: Macromedia.

Drucker, Peter F. (1988, January-February). The coming of the new organization. *Harvard Business Review*, pp. 45-53.

Electronic Arts. (2004). *The Sims* [Web site for suite of computer/videogames]. < http://thesims.ea.com/us/index.html?menu = about&content = about/index.html > .

Faust and Shortee. [Web site]. (n.d./2004). < http://www.faustandshortee.com. >

Feenberg, Andrew. (1997). *The critical theory of technology*. Oxford: Oxford University Press.

The Flaming Lips. (1997). *Zaireeka* [CD Box Set.] Burbank, CA: Warner Bros.

The Flaming Lips. (1998). Boombox No. 13 Handout. PDF version available at < http://download.wbr.com/flaminglips/PDF/bbe160598handout.pdf > .

The Flaming Lips. [Web site]. (2004). < http://www.flaminglips.com. >

Foucault, Michel. (1977). "What is an author?" In Donald F. Bouchard (Ed.), *Language, Counter-Memory, Practice: Selected Essays and Interviews* (Donald F. Bouchard & Sherry Simon, Trans.) (pp. 113-138). Ithaca, NY: Cornell University Press.

Foucault, Michel. (1986, Spring). Of Other Spaces In *Diacritics*, (Jay Miskowiec, Trans.), (pp. 22-27). [Original work published 1984]

Fraunfelder, Mark, Cory Doctorow, David Pescovitz, and Xeni Jardin (Eds.). (n.d./2004). *Boingboing: A directory of wonderful things*. < http://www.boingboing.net/ > .

Gadd, Mike. (2004, April 4). Skratchcon2000 Report. *Youth Radio*. < http://www.youthradio.org/music/001001_skratchcon.shtml. >

Gibson, William. (1984). *Neuromancer*. New York: Ace Books.

Google. [Web site]. (April 4, 2004). < http://www.google.com. >

Grandmaster Flash. (1981). The adventures of grandmaster flash on the wheels of steel. Englewood, NJ: Sugar Hill Records. [Rpt. in Grandmaster Flash, The Furious Five, and Grandmaster Mel. (1999). *Back to the Old School* [CD Box Set]. London: Sequence Records.)

Grossberg, Larry. (1993, March). Cultural studies and/in new worlds. *Critical Studies in Mass Communication, 10*(1), 1-22.

Grossberg, Larry (Ed.). (1996). On postmodernism and articulation: An interview with Stuart Hall. In David Morley and Kuan-Hsing Chen (Eds.), *Stuart Hall: Critical Dialogues in Cultural Studies*. New York: Routledge. [Rpt. from *Journal of Communication Inquiry* (1986), 10(2), 45-60.]

Grossberg, Lawrence, and Jennifer Daryl Slack. (1985). An introduction to Stuart Hall's essay [Introduction to Hall, 1985.] *Critical Studies in Mass Communication, 2*, 87-90.

Hall, Stuart. (1983). The problem of ideology: Marxism without guarantees. In Betty Matthews (Ed.), *Marx 100 years on* (pp. 57-85). London: Lawrence & Wishart.

Hall, Stuart. (1985, June). Signification, representation, ideology: Althusser and the post-structuralist debates. *Critical Studies in Mass Communication, 2*, 91-114.

Hall, Stuart. (1989). Ideology and communication theory. In Lawrence Grossberg, Brenda Dervin, Barbara J. O'Keefe, & Ellen Wartella (Eds.), *Rethinking communication: Vol. 1. Paradigm issues* (pp. 40-52). Newbury Park: Sage.

Hebdige, Dick. (1989). *Hiding in the light: On images and things*. London: Comedia.

Holmevick, Jan Rune, and Cynthia Haynes. (2004, April 4). *enCore Xpress*. < http://lingua.utdallas.edu/encore/. >

Internet Explorer: Mac (Version 5.2). (2001). Redmond, WA: Microsoft.

Issacs, Ellen. (2003, November). A closer look at our common wisdom. *ACM Queue*, 1(8). [Web site]. < http://www.acmqueue.com/modules.php?name = Content&pa = showpage&pid = 91 > .

Jameson, Frederic. (1991). *Postmodernism: Or, the cultural logic of late capitalism*. Durham, NC: Duke University Press.

Janecek. (n.d./2004). Flaming Lips Parking Lot Experiments [Web page]. < http://www.janecek.com/parkinglot.html > .

Johnson, Jeff. (n.d./2004). The Parking Lot Experiment. [Web page]. < http://www.wbr.com/flaminglips/cmp/parking.htm > .

Johnson-Eilola, Johndan. (1996). Relocating the value of work: Technical communication in a post-industrial age. *Technical Communication Quarterly, 5*(3), 245-270.

Johnson-Eilola, Johndan. (1997). Living on the surface: Learning in the age of global communication networks. In Ilana Snyder (Ed.), *Taking literacy into the electronic age* (pp. 185-210). Melbourne, Australia: Allen and Unwin; New York: Routledge.

Johnson-Eilola, Johndan. (1999, March). Space | action | movement: Understanding composition as architecture. Conference on College Composition and Communication. Available at < http://www.clarkson.edu/ ~ johndan//read/ architecture/welcome.html > .

Joyce, Michael Thomas. (1996). The momentary advantage of our awkwardness. In Michael Joyce (Ed.), *Of two minds: Hypertext pedagogy poetics* (pp. 220-226). Ann Arbor: University of Michigan Press.

Katz, Jonathan. (n.d./2004, April 4). *The WWW virtual punchcard (Punch Card) Server*. < http://www.facade.com/legacy/punchcard/. >

Koolhaas, Rem, Stefano Boeri, Sanford Kwinter, Nadia Tazi, and Daniela Fabricus. (2001). *Mutations*. Bourdeaux: ACTAR.

Korot, Beryl. (2002). Dachau 1974. In S. Reich (Ed.). (2002). *Writings on music, 1965-2000* (pp. 85-86). Cambridge, England: Oxford University Press.

Kubrick, Stanley (Producer and Director). (1971). *A clockwork orange*. Burbank, CA: Warner Bros.

Kushner, Donald (Producer), and Steven Lisberger (Director). (1982). *Tron*. Burbank, CA: Disney.

Lab Answers IM Questions. (2003, April 14). *eWeek* [Web site]. < http://www.eweek. com/article2/0,1759,1023574,00.asp > .

Louderback, Jim. (2003, July 31). New uses for instant messaging. *eWeek* [Web site]. < http://www.eweek.com/article2/0,4149,1208140,00.asp > .

Lynch, Kevin. (2004). *Internet applications: A new frontier*. San Francisco, CA: Macromedia. PDF file available at < http://www.macromedia.com/ software/central/whitepaper/central_wp.pdf. >

Lyotard, Jean-François. (1984). *The postmodern condition: A report on knowledge* (Geoff Bennington & Brian Massumi, Trans.). Minneapolis: University of Minnesota Press.

Microsoft Finland. (2004). Where do you want to go today? [Web site]. < http://www.microsoft.com/finland/info/comppres/default.asp > .

Microsoft Word X for Mac. (2001). Redmond, WA: Microsoft.

Milchan, Arnon (Producer) and Terry Gilliam, (Director). (1985). *Brazil*. Hollywood, CA: Universal Pictures.

Mirel, Barbara. (1996). Writing and database technology: Extending the definition of writing in the workplace. In Patricia Sullivan & Jennie Dautermann (Eds.), *Electronic Literacies in the Workplace: Technologies of Writing*. Urbana, IL: NCTE; Houghton, MI: Computers & Composition.

Mirel, Barbara. (2003). *Interaction design for complex problem solving*. Amsterdam: Elsevier/Morgan Kaufman.

Mitchell, William J. (1996). *City of bits: space, place, and the infobahn*. Cambridge, MA: MIT Press.

Molen, Gerald R., Bonnie Curtis, Walter F. Parkes, Jan de Bont (Producers), and Steven Speilberg (Director). (2002). *Minority report*. Universal City, CA: 20th Century Fox and Dreamworks SKG.

Moore, Michael (Producer and Director). (1989). *Roger and me*. Burbank, CA: Warner Bros.

Morley, David. (1996). EurAm, modernity, reason and alterity: Or, postmodernism, the highest stage of cultural imperialism? In David Morley & Kuan-Hsing Chen (Eds.), *Stuart Hall: Critical Dialogues in Cultural Studies*. New York: Routledge. [Rpt. from *Journal of Communication Inquiry* (1986), 10(2), 326-360.]

Nardi, Bonnie A. and Vicki L. O'Day. (2000). *Information ecologies: Using technology with heart*. Cambridge, MA: MIT Press.

National Telecommunications and Information Administration. (n.d./2004). Falling through the net: defining the digital divide [Web site]. < http://www.ntia. doc.gov/ntiahome/fttn99/contents.html > .

Noon, Jeff. (2002). *Falling out of cars*. London: Transword.

Norman, Donald. (1988). *The psychology of everyday things*. New York: Basic Books.

Per.Oxyd. (1995). Cambridge, MA: Dongleware USA.

Pfau, Peter and Wes Jones. (1987). Untitled. In Robert McCarter (Ed.), *Building: Machines* (pp. 42-60). New York: Pamphlet Architecture and Princeton Architectural Press.

Ranchero Software. (2003). *NetNewsWire Pro* (Version 1.0.8). Seattle, WA: Author.

Rappaport, Daniel, Michael Rotenberg (Producers), and Mike Judge (Director). (1999). *Office space*. Universal City, CA: 20th Century Fox.

Reich, Robert B. (1991). *The work of nations: Preparing ourselves for 21st-century capitalism*. New York: Alfred A. Knopf.

Reich, Robert (2001). *The future of success*. New York: Alfred A. Knopf.

Reich, Steve. (2002). *Writings on music, 1965-2000*. Cambridge, England: Oxford University Press.

Reighley, Kurt B. (2000). *Looking for the perfect beat: The art and culture of the DJ*. New York: Pocket Books/MTV Books.

Rodriguez, Richard (Producer and Director). (2002). *Inside troublemaker studios*. New York: Columbia Pictures.

Ronell, Avital. (1989). *The telephone book: Technology, schizophrenia, electric speech*. Lincoln: University of Nebraska Press.

Rosenfeld, Louis, and Peter Moreville. (2002). *Information architecture for the World Wide Web: Designing large-scale web sites* (2nd ed.). Sebastopol, CA: O'Reilly.

Selber, Stuart A. (2004). *Multiliteracies for a digital age*. Carbondale: Southern Illinois University Press.

Shannon, Claude E. & Warren Weaver. (1949). *The mathematical theory of communication*, Urbana: University of Illinois Press.

Slack, Jennifer Daryl. (1996). The theory and method of articulation in cultural studies. In David Morley & Kuan-Hsing Chen (Eds.), *Stuart Hall: Critical dialogues in cultural studies*. New York: Routledge. [Rpt. from *Journal of Communication Inquiry* (1986), 10(2), 112-130.]

Spinuzzi, Clay. (2003). *Tracing genres through organizations: A sociocultural approach to information design*. Cambridge, MA: MIT Press.

Taylor, Todd, & Halbritter, Scott (2003, March 20). "New Media Composition Live." Conference on College Composition and Communication, New York.

Theroux, Paul. (1992). *The happy isles of Oceania: Paddling the Pacific*. New York: Ballantine.

Thumbs down for text messages—They are official addictive. (2003, October 5). *The Telegraph* (U.K.). < http://www.telegraph.co.uk/news/main.jhtml?xml = %2Fnews%2F2003%2F10%2F05%2Fntxt05.xml >

Tschumi, Bernard. (1995). The Manhattan transcripts: Theoretical projects. London: Academy Editions.

Tschumi, Bernard. (1996). *Architecture and disjunction*. Cambridge, MA: MIT Press.

Tufte, Edward. (2003, September). PowerPoint is Evil. *Wired* 11(09) [Web site]. <
   http://www.wired.com/wired/archive/11.09/ppt2.html >.

Virilio, Paul. (1997). *Pure war*. New York: Autonomedia/Semiotext(e).

VisiCalc. (1979). Arlington, MA: Software Arts.

Wigley, Mark. (1995). *The architecture of deconstruction: Derrida's haunt*.
   Cambridge, MA: MIT Press.

The Wired Diaries. (1999, January). *Wired* 7(01) [Jan. 1999]. < http://www.wired.
   com/wired/archive/7.01/diaries.html?pg = 1 &topic = &topic_set = >

"Young prefer texting to calls." (2003, June 13). *BBC News (U.K. Edition)*.
   < http://news.bbc.co.uk/1/hi/business/2985072.stm >.

Zuboff, Shoshana. (1989). *In the age of the smart machine: The future of work and
   power*. New York: Basic Books.

AUTHOR INDEX

SUBJECT INDEX

A

Abstraction, for symbolic analysts, 30
Acceptable meanings, articulations as
    suggestions about, 89
Access to information, 122-123
Active production, 129
Adobe PageMaker, 68-69
Adobe Photoshop, 1
Adventure (UNIX game), 54
*The Adventures of Grandmaster Flash
    on the Wheels of Steel,* 114
Affordances, 21
Ambivalent theories of technology, 21
AOL, IM in, 90
Architecture, deconstructivist, of infor-
    mation, 108
Architecture of Deconstruction, The,
    124-125
Articulation theory, 18, 23-32, 102
    postmodernism in relation to, 126
Articulation workers, education of, 98
Articulations, 7, 21, 24, 58
    both material and symbolic, 83
    changing, of interface design, 33-38,
        90
    of communication, 58
    contingent, 20
    continued processes of, 34, 102
    in the datacloud, 89-106
    of interfaces, 58
    as a process of creating connections,
        26
    as suggestions about acceptable
        meanings, 89
    See also Disarticulations;
        Rearticulations

Artifacts, breaking down, 126
Assumptions, of order and certainty,
    123
AT&T Labs, 95, 139
Audio editing environments, nonlinear,
    3

B

Bambatta, Afrikaa, 113-114
Battlesounds, 142
"Belongingness," 7
Black, Matt, 141
Blade Runner, 15-16
Blondie, 114
BoingBoing, 130
Boombox Experiment, 115, 117
    handout for, 108-109
Brant, Henry, 118
Brazil, 11-14, 52, 74
    information society in, 13
    office technologies in, 12
Breakdowns, 31
    as the first phase of rebuilding, 16
    and recombination, 17-19
    seen as bad, 24
    of subjectivities, 26
    turntablism and, 109-115
Browsers, history menu in, 106n
Bubonic plague, in nursery rhymes, 8
Buildings, as performances enacted by
    their occupants, 126-127
Burstein, Laura, 9
Byrne, David, 100

C

Cage, John, 142
Capitalism, 4
    postindustrial, 4

Printed in the United States
29583LVS00001B/67-135

9 781572 736344